ECHO ISLAND

Echo Island

A NOVEL

EDWARD KARLOW

ISBNs: 978-0-9979471-0-6 (paperback); 978-0-9979471-1-3 (ePub); 978-0-9979471-2-0 (Kindle)

Printed in the United States of America
First Printing: 2017
21 20 19 18 17 5 4 3 2 1

Cover photography by Brandon Eckroth, brandoneckroth.com
Cover and interior design by Ryan Scheife, Mayfly Design, mayflydesign.com
Cover models: Josh Zwick, zwick045@umn.edu and Riley L.

To order, visit edwardkarlow.com

For

Moso
Jeanne & Maurice
Björk Guðmundsdóttir
Daryl Hannah
Ernest Oberholtzer
&
Agnès Varda

Friday, July 8th

I spent almost five hours in a Vehicle of the Oppressor: my parents' gigantic gas-guzzling sports utility vehicle. It was oppressing me and our little planet as I sat next to my older brother, Derek. He and I tried to get along, but we were brother and sister, so we fought and argued.

"Reesie, are you thinking about all the fossil fuels we're using on this trip?" he asked.

"Who's Reesie?"

"You, Theresa, the prima diva," he teased.

"You're so original," I argued back.

"So, are you obsessing about gas mileage or what?" He pushed the subject more.

"No, I'm not," I responded.

"I knew it! You can't hide it. It's written all over your face," he gloated and went back to studying graphs and numbers on his laptop.

Like I said, Derek and I fought a little. Okay, we were constantly tearing each other apart verbally, but brothers and sisters were designed that way. Right?

Blatherskite. That was the name I gave him. I study weird, outdated scientific words, mostly to make Derek annoyed with me. A blatherskite was a person who talked at great length without making much sense. He was most definitely one.

Anyhow, our parents drove us north of the city, into the middle of the woods, where there were gigantic pine trees and empty windy roads. We even passed a small bait shop that sold worms and minnows and beer. Everyone drove pick-ups and there were handmade signs for boat storage and snowmobile repairs every mile.

My mom insisted that we blast the air conditioning, but I cracked the window for fresh air that wasn't all smoggy, like in the city.

I'm so sick of pollution and plastic and the way everyone treats our planet, tired of being fifteen and having all the adults in my life tell me what to do, but turn around and watch the Earth be destroyed. But who was I to say what was right? And who wanted to hear me lecture? Nobody likes to be preached at. Plus, I don't even know who I am. I'm still trying to figure that out.

I don't really fit in with one group, I know that much at least. Part of me gets along with the athletic group because I'm outdoorsy, but the other part of me wants to go "goth," because there's so much doom and gloom to be found. I'm not ready for black lipstick, but I'm not ready to join a sorority either.

I don't own one of those remove-your-makeup headbands that some girls wear. I'm not a fashion-obsessed pink-polka-dot-wearing girl. Definitely not. I don't think I've worn a dress since I was six. I like to think I could fit in with all groups or cliques or whatever, but in reality, I don't fit in with any of them.

So I take a little from each group and make it my own. I like black combat boots and extra eyeliner, but I also can be found in an outdoorsy fleece jacket and a bike helmet. It confuses people (including myself) when you don't fit neatly into one specific box. I try to place myself outside the box. I don't know. It isn't easy. That's probably why I only have one good friend, Brooke. We've been friends since we were five. We bonded by studying worms and insects on the kickball field. The classic we're-both-nerdy-outcasts-so-le t's-stick-together style friendship. Being a nerdy outcast, I've only had one ex-boyfriend, Trevor. More about him later. I shouldn't have even brought him up.

My parents are dropping Derek and me off at my Aunt Kat's house on the island, where we'll be staying for almost two weeks. Kat's real name is Katherine, but only my mom calls her that. Mom and Dad are going on a rich-fancy-friend cabin thing where they don't want two teenagers hanging around. A short escape for my parents' latest obsessions in the city.

I didn't know it, but my life was about to do a complete 180 from where I was in the back seat with my brother. There was no way I could have known I was a week away from risking my life. That I would see so many things I couldn't believe were real. That I would discover secrets that weren't just dangerous but truly magical.

And that I was going to feel something for someone, an event that I had only read about. I was about to actually live an exciting, wild life instead of watching others' adventurous lives from the sidelines.

But back to my Aunt Kat. She's nothing like my parents: she's fun and cares a lot about the little island she lives on up in the woods. She's fit, has a couple tattoos, wears cut-off jeans, plaid shirts, and a beat-up straw hat. It's even rumored that she won some kind of beer drinking contest at the Sturgis Motorcycle Rally in South Dakota when she was younger.

"That was twenty years ago," she'd always say when I'd ask her for details on her beer championship.

"Please tell me," I'd plead.

"It was rock bands and beer, that's all I will say about my wild days. Now it's more kale and quinoa."

"Maybe when I'm older, you can tell me?" I'd ask.

"Perhaps," she'd respond.

Now, she owns her own supper club, Kat's Club, and everyone on Echo Island knows her. She's not detached and afraid to talk to her neighbors like my upstanding leader-type parents, the lovely Jim and Linda Clarke. And she didn't freak out when I told her that I was a vegetarian, or that I once chained myself to a tree to protest some new condos, or that I saved my yogurt containers to re-use for my leftovers.

Aunt Kat visits us in the city about once a year. She stays with us and makes my parents a little nutty with her unconventional ways. She cooks us crazy healthy meals and brings progressive ideas into our home. Once, she even planted an entire vegetable garden on our front yard while my parents were at work. That was a memorable visit for our suburban street. Each time, she'd demand that we come back to the island and visit her. We had just never found the time until this year.

Who am I? I'm Theresa Clark. I'm fifteen. I like science and saving the environment. I'm not into love and romance and testosterone-filled boys who pretend they're already men.

I was into love and romance for a little bit. His name was

Trevor Jacobson. I didn't like Trevor at first, but then he grew on me. And by the time I really liked him, he decided he didn't want to see me anymore. He wanted to see Brenda Jenson instead. Brenda Jenson was nice and blond and smelled like expensive perfume. I wasn't always that nice, not blond, and I didn't like spraying myself with expensive chemicals.

Thinking about him or even saying his name made my stomach hurt. I had already lost enough sleep over him. So romance? I was going to pass on that for a little while. Maybe a long while.

My best friend Brooke and I have our own movement, called the "Earth's Last Chance Club." We're the only two members, but we're super active. We set up a table once a week at the grocery store to encourage people to recycle their plastic, glass, and paper. Successful or popular? No. But it's what we do. I sometimes get us in trouble, but Brooke gets us out of it. She's smart and her thick-rimmed glasses give her an authority that adults trust.

I started wearing a fork necklace around town recently, sort of like carrying your own water bottle. It's just a metal fork with a hole drilled in it and a chain. That way, I don't have to use plastic forks when I eat out. I pretend it's my badge of honor, a way to show I support the planet. I hope to start a revolution of fork necklace wearers, but I'm not sure it's working.

My brother Derek thinks it's gross, but he's only interested in studying business management or investment banking or something. What was grosser than that? Plus, I wash the fork all the time, so it's not really that gross. Plastic forks winding up in our oceans and rivers? That's what's gross to me.

What was doing on Echo Island? Waiting tables at Kat's Club. My brother was going to balance her books or figure out a business plan or something business-like and boring. He was good with numbers. I was too, but I had bigger fish to fry.

We stopped at a small gas station in the middle of nowhere and hopped out to stretch. Derek grabbed another can of soda and threw the plastic six-pack ring on the ground.

Besides gigantic gas-guzzling cars, those plastic six-pack rings were another big enemy of mine—a sign of the apocalypse. I've already lectured him on what those six-pack rings can do to animals if they get one stuck around their necks. I picked it up and put it in my pocket, so I could cut it up and recycle it later.

"There it is," my mom said and pointed.

"The lake?" I asked.

"The lake, yes. And Echo Island. Way out there, see?"

I shielded my eyes from the sun and observed the lake. We could only see a sliver of it, because there were pine trees everywhere, but I could see the island, miles away. It looked like a little dot on the big lake.

I crossed the street to get a better look at the island. I saw a figure, a guy waterskiing. I focused on him as if I had used a telescope. He seemed around my age, and he stared me right in the eye for a second. He went by so fast, but his intense eye contact caught me off guard. I couldn't tell what was going on. It didn't look like he was wearing skis. He had a bright-colored swimsuit, that's about all I could tell.

"What are you looking at?" Derek surprised me. I jumped a little.

"Quit sneaking up on me!" I complained.

"What's out there?" he asked.

"A guy waterskiing with no water skis."

"It's called barefooting, genius. I thought you knew every outdoorsy sport there was," he teased.

"What's going on?" My mom joined us.

"Theresa thinks she saw someone barefooting, but I don't hear a boat or anything. I think the fresh air's gone to her brain," he said.

"Funny, fresh air helps you think better, it doesn't make you hallucinate," I responded.

"I think you were seeing things," my mom added.

"Huh?" I said, slightly annoyed.

"This part of the lake doesn't allow motorized boats—" she answered, but was interrupted by Derek, the Neanderthal: "What the hell's with all this ash in the air?" We all looked up to see campfire ash floating in the sky.

"Let's get out of here, before we have to breathe this crap into our lungs," Derek complained.

"For once you're interested in the air quality?" I said.

"Whatever, get over yourself," he retorted. My mom rolled her eyes at our bickering and they both hopped into the car. I started to follow, but turned again to watch the ash float to the ground. I held my hand out and a piece of ash landed on it. It had a light blue tint to it. I looked closer. It was a snowflake.

"Snow?" I whispered to myself. How could it be snowing in mid-July? I squeezed my hand shut to see if it would melt in my palm. I opened my hand back up and it had melted. *It really was snow!* I thought to myself.

I hopped back in the car next to my brother. "Doesn't that look like snow out there?" I asked, afraid to admit that it had just melted in my hand.

"Snow in July? Right," Derek said and covered his ears with his headphones.

"It could be snow," my mom said. "Your Aunt Katherine says this lake has magic powers."

"What?" I asked. "Do you think it does?"

"I believe in the magic of online shopping and free shipping, not magic lakes," she said.

I touched the window and watched all the ash or snow or whatever it was disappear as we drove away.

"When I was younger, I used to think the island was magic," my mom said, out of the blue. "Weird stuff has always happened to me there, I have to admit. And I've had the most vivid dreams of my life at your aunt's house," my mom added and stared out the window. She opened it and held out her hand to play with the wind.

I said my goodbyes to my parents and settled in here in Aunt Kat's attic guest bedroom. Derek wanted the big guest room, but that's okay, because I like attics. I stayed in this attic when I was five and loved it even then. This cozy attic was one of my earliest memories of my entire life. I could recall little from when I was five, but this room and this feeling I remembered.

Echo Island was a lot smaller than I thought it was. There was one major road that circles it and a round trip would only be about five miles. There wasn't a bunch to do here, but I guess that's why older people liked it. They're able to relax.

It was easy to find a beach; they were all over the place.

Kat's Club was one of the most popular spots and everyone on the island seemed to love her.

My parents used to be a lot closer to Aunt Kat and we stayed here once as a family. I think she was too much of a rebel for them. She did her own thing and said whatever she wanted; she wasn't afraid of anything or anyone.

Our family was always too busy to come up to the island after we got older, so we stayed in the toxic polluted city.

"Someone has to pay for the roof over your head," my always-wearing-khakis dad would say.

Then my mom would add, "We can't all be like Aunt Katherine, camping out in the woods, doing whatever we want and eating nuts and twigs and berries."

Echo Island wasn't a place I should have liked, but I loved it when I was five and I fell back in love once the island came into view from the water. I was a science and nature girl, but I lived in the city. There was so much open space here. So much water and so much nature. I spend a lot of time fighting for nature, but in truth, I didn't spent too much time *in* nature.

Aunt Kat had electricity and warm water, but there was no mall, movie theater, or car dealership on the island. As you might have guessed, I wasn't into malls. Aunt Kat said there was only one spot on the island to get a good cell phone signal, but I didn't have many people to text, except for Brooke. She was back in the city, fighting the good fight for our club.

New boys? There were no boys to text. Boys were annoying and distracting and after Trevor, I needed a break. It's all so obvious what was going on in their brains. I've read all about it and it all boiled down to a scientific explanation. Like kissing. Even kissing was science; I had studied it. I read that kissing was a way for the male to pass on testosterone to the female. Her libido would spike and that would lead to more kissing and then babies and a family.

It was all science and it all could be explained. Science was magic without all the lies. People called it magic or romance or love, but I've read it boiled down to three stages:

1. Lust
2. Attraction
3. Attachment

It was only a bunch of chemicals flying around in your brain: dopamine, serotonin, oxytocin, and vasopression. The "Love Lock" bridge in Paris? All these lovey-dovey couples attaching padlocks of love to the sides of a poor little bridge. Gobs and gobs of padlocks from couples. So many that they almost made the bridge collapse. Forty-five tons of locks! City workers had to risk their lives removing the bridge's panels.

What did love do for us? It was plain dangerous and should be avoided if you ask me. Look how much work I could've gotten done if I wasn't at home, sad and depressed over Trevor. Where did it get me?

Okay, off to bed. Not another word about Trevor or love or dopamine or Paris.

Saturday, July 9th

I woke up early today in the little attic at Aunt Kat's. It was so quiet the previous night that I almost couldn't sleep, but I woke up the way I did when I was a little kid—completely rested and to the aroma of blueberry pancakes. The blueberries grew wild up there, so they're fresh and tasty. A city girl, like me, didn't expect to go for a stroll and come back with breakfast.

My brother wasn't up yet, so Aunt Kat and I let him sleep and took a long walk along the beach. I found a bunch of cans and bottles littered there.

"The battle continues," she said as she pulled out a trash bag from her pocket. "I clean up whenever I'm here. It makes me feel better." I picked up some garbage and helped her on her quest. I understand Aunt Kat and she understands me in a way my parents don't.

"It's so good to have you back on Echo," she said.

"It's great to be back, it's just..." I stopped myself. I didn't want to offend her, but I didn't remember much of the island. It had been, like, a decade since I was on it.

"Just what?" Aunt Kat asked nicely.

"I don't remember much from when I was five."

"Oh, I get it. You will. Give it time," she said nicely. I thought about what my mom said and had to ask Kat.

"Does the island really have magic powers?"

"Where did you hear that?" Aunt Kat asked.

"Mom told me there were rumors."

"Your mom did? Well, if she says so," she teased. She gave me a small smile as if she wanted to tell me more, but we walked in silence instead.

"C'mon, let's go say hi to Mooshy," she finally said.

We passed a gigantic statue of an elk made out of black iron or bronze or some kind of sturdy metal.

"Do you remember Mooshy?" she asked me.

"I don't think so. Mooshy?" I said. "Like, mushy?"

"Mooshy is short for Omashkooz. It means 'elk' in Ojibwa."

I knocked on the statue of Mooshy and it made a deep, hollow metal sound back at me.

"He's been guarding the island for a long time. He greets everyone who hops off that ferry and reminds them of the power of nature. Don't you think?" Aunt Kat asked.

I agreed and we kept going. I looked back at the statue and studied it. It seemed bigger than life, but was it supposed to be? Was the real Mooshy bigger than an average elk?

"Some older people on the island say Mooshy is real and that he will live forever. I thought I saw him once, but . . ." Aunt Kat stopped herself.

"You thought you saw Mooshy?" I asked. "The eternal elk?" I said and laughed a little.

"Don't make fun. You might spot him in the next week, just be warned. People talk about him, young people too. It's not just the old ladies with bad vision who have caught a glimpse of him," Aunt Kat explained.

"Maybe you saw Mooshy's grandson or something," I offered.

"Maybe. Either way, the elk I saw was gigantic, and—"

"What?"

"Nothing."

"I won't make fun, I promise," I pleaded.

"Don't tell your mom I said this, but it seemed like Mooshy was saying something to me, that he knew who I was."

I took one last glance at Mooshy the Elk to determine if the statue would say something to me, but he didn't.

I understand I've seen too many movies, but I had the sense that his eyes were real and that at any second, he would turn his regal face toward mine and shock me right out of my shoes.

That's when we ran into Lily, the dishwasher from Kat's Club; I had noticed her earlier at my restaurant training session. She was a little younger than me, and her hair was bright orange and her skin was very pale. She had big hazel eyes that were too intense for someone her age. Her cheeks sort of glowed from within. It was safe to say that Lily was quite possibly the most striking teenage dishwasher in the world. If that wasn't enough, she was sporty and seemed so natural in a swimsuit.

Don't even get me started on wearing swimsuits. Uggghhh. I only brought one swimsuit, my trusty black one-piece, but that didn't mean I would be caught in it that often. Anyhow, back to Lily. Aunt Kat had to ask her a ton of questions to get her to talk.

"What are you up to? How's your Grandpa Thomas?

Where's your brother? What else do you have planned for the day?" Aunt Kat asked Lily.

Lily answered with a few words. She smiled pleasantly and moved toward the beach. She started to swim underwater. I couldn't see where she came up for air, so I panicked.

"Where did Lily go?" I said. Aunt Kat looked out to the gigantic lake and saw her head pop up.

"There she is, way out there. How did she swim so fast?" she asked. I replied while squinting to find Lily, "I don't know."

"She lives for swimming," she added, then said, "The flyers! I forgot about the flyers for the Blue Moon Dance next week. Will you help me post them?"

"Of course," I replied, but thought, *Please don't make me go to the dance!* I was dreading the Blue Moon Dance because Aunt Kat was a sponsor and I knew I'd have to dress up for it. My mom made me pack a nice dress, but I totally hated wearing dresses.

The town was so small, I knew if I wore my usual black T-shirt and heavy eyeliner, the people in town would chase me through the streets with torches. I can't believe I was there for just over a week and it happened to be during the big summer dance.

I don't dance.

I don't like dancing.

Watching other people dance makes me nervous.

"You're going to have so much fun at the dance," Aunt Kat offered.

"I don't really dance, though . . ."

"Everyone dances. Don't worry about it," she said. The only time I dance is alone in my room with headphones on, but that rarely happens.

We made it back to the house to get the flyers and found Derek wandering around with his laptop. I told him that he looked like a robot.

"I'm trying to get a wi-fi signal, what would you know? Like, stay out of it," he hissed at me.

I ignored him, which made him more frustrated. He usually wants me to fight back, but being silent is my way of fighting back, because it's what bugs him the most.

"Follow me, Derek," Aunt Kat said. "I'll show you the best wi-fi spot in the whole house."

"I'm going back into town to hang up the flyers," I yelled as they left the room.

"Take my bike if you'd like, honey!" she said.

Aunt Kat had an old one-speed bike with a basket on the handlebars. I threw the flyers in the basket and took off. For the first time in a long time, I had so much energy. I could feel the sun and the wind and the trees, they were all fueling my bike ride. The sun felt different up on the island. It felt crisp and comforting, and more like it belonged to me.

Before I knew it, I had biked the loop that goes around the entire island. Along the ride, I saw small wood cabins and new fancy lake homes on the "wealthier side" of the island. I also passed a little dive bar called the Echo Oasis, the marina, a gift store, three other restaurants, a coffee shop, a teeny tiny bait shop, a couple beachfront hotels, and a convenience store.

All along the way, I taped and stapled up flyers for the Blue Moon Dance. I felt like hiding all the flyers. Why would I want more people to see me at a dance? I put them up anyway, and as I said before, I did it for Aunt Kat.

I don't know how she and my mom can be sisters, when my mom is such a materialist shopper and Aunt Kat's so cool.

I'm lucky to have her in my life. Not too many adults really look me in the eye and listen to what I have to say. Aunt Kat does that. My parents usually give me a look that says, *How long until she's done talking so I can go back to my charts and stocks and coffee and scotch and plastic storage bins?*

I know I'm not officially an adult and all, but I have ideas and I want to share them. So many people say stuff like, "Oh, it's complicated," and, "That's terrible. How can we do that to another human? How can we do that to the planet?" Then they turn the page of the newspaper, or click the window closed on their computer, and go to bed.

All my teachers at school say we should think critically, but if you really did, you'd go insane with all the injustices in the world. Sometimes I wonder, how can we all get out of bed in the morning? I even came across a word for this feeling once: kuebiko.

Kuebiko means a state of exhaustion inspired by acts of senseless violence. Pollution to me is violence against the Earth. How can we all get in our cars and drive off and pollute the Earth with how we live?

The beauty of the woods, the island, and the gigantic lake really got to me, I guess. I locked up my bike and went back to the beach, my mind racing with ideas. That's when I saw it: an old tire had washed up on the beach. I looked around and saw more trash: beer cans, bottles, empty cigarette packs, part of a plastic patio chair, and a lot more.

I could feel my face flush with anger. I grabbed the tire and carried it back to the town square. A couple people saw me and asked if I needed help.

"Thanks, I'm okay," I said and trudged along. Something

popped into my brain—a secret. I stashed the tire in the bushes when nobody was looking.

My secret: I had a plan for the tire and all the other trash on the beach, but I wouldn't be able to do it until late at night. I worked my way back to Aunt Kat's, scheming the whole way.

I acted naturally around Derek and Aunt Kat and eventually went to bed. I set my alarm for three in the morning with my plan whirling in my brain as I fell asleep. It was difficult to fall asleep with all the outcomes I was imagining for my mission.

I woke up to the alarm at three in the morning and set out on Aunt Kat's bike. I was a little groggy, but the night's air felt so new, even the water smelled fresh. I felt energized by the night—it seemed so alive.

I gathered all the trash from the beach under the light from the almost-full moon. Trash bag after trash bag, I took all the trash I could find, then the tire, and dragged the bags over to the Mooshy the Elk statue.

I looked around and after feeling confident I was alone, I started hanging all the trash from Mooshy's antlers, over his back, and from his tail. I had to toss a lot onto Mooshy and hope it landed somewhere it would stay. There were a lot of plastic bags, so those were easy to get trapped onto his antlers. It took several tosses, but I was able to hook the tire to his antler too. This was my statement: *Look at what we have all done to this beautiful animal, to nature.*

I stepped back to look at my handiwork and was shocked by it. It was five in the morning and poor Mooshy looked so sad, but still so noble with all of *our* junk on his back. All the junk including one half-rotten turkey sandwich in its plastic gas station wrapper.

Suddenly, I heard a noise behind me. I spun around, terrified, but saw nothing. Something odd happened, though. The odor of the sandwich was replaced by the scent of a fresh lake, sorta like the scent of my hair drying in the sun after swimming. It was something I could both smell and almost touch. I took a deep breath and looked around, but eventually biked away.

Back in bed, my head collapsed onto my pillow and I fell asleep pretty fast. My little activist statement ran through my brain.

Does this island have a newspaper?

Will my statement be front-page news?

Will people grasp what they're doing to the planet?

Will it make the news down in the city?

Will my secret be discovered?

Sunday, July 10th

I didn't have my first work shift until lunch, so I was able to sleep through breakfast. I couldn't wait to take the bike past Mooshy the Elk and discover what a commotion I had caused with the trash. I pictured the locals staring up at it, taking pictures, news reporters and more.

As I got closer to the town square, I had a strange inkling. Where were all the outraged people? I saw an elderly couple and they just smiled at me.

I arrived at the Mooshy statue and couldn't believe what had happened: all the trash was gone. He looked better than before. The weeds were pulled and he looked even shinier. Did the locals clean it all up without realizing the message?

Disappointed, I went to the supper club. Aunt Kat wanted to start me out with only one customer. Sadly, that customer was my brother. Wow, this had shaped up to be one of the lamest days of my life. Derek demanded that he get all his food in to-go containers with plastic lids.

"But you're eating here, right?" I asked with a touch of anger.

"Yeah, but you never know. I might want to leave at some

point." *So the Earth gets to pay the price for all his stupid whims? Not on my shift!*

"You're not getting a bunch of plastic because you're too dumb to figure out whether or not you can sit here for ten minutes and shove food into your face!" I replied, the way only a younger sister can reply.

"I'd like to see the manager," he said.

"Get all the plastic you want, you caveman, but get it yourself!" I said in a mean whisper.

Then I thought of something. I returned to his table and reported, "Kat's Club only has biodegradable to-go containers, so you're out of luck, Derek!" Dramatic, I know. I stormed off to the kitchen and locked myself in the dessert cooler.

I was mid-bite in a slice of death by chocolate cake when Lily opened the door.

"Oh sorry, Theresa," she said sweetly. I told her it was okay. I offered her a slice of cake, but she refused.

"Everything okay?" she asked.

I replied, "I'm so over my idiot brother out there. I sincerely hope you don't have an older brother who assumes he knows everything."

She replied, "I do have a brother; his name is Max."

She told me how she and Max live with their grandfather Thomas by the Echo Oasis bar. And how their grandfather was the owner of the bar.

"He's the one who has the baby deer," she added.

"Oh, my aunt told me about Thomas. He seems like a special guy. You're lucky."

"I am. He's very good to us," she responded.

"What about your brother? Is he a moron like mine?" I asked.

She replied, "No, he's nice. I like him a lot."

I moaned and complained, "Who likes their brother?"

She replied innocently like it was a real question, "I do."

I clearly wasn't having a "we hate our brothers" bonding moment with Lily. What planet was she from? I changed the subject.

"Will you help me take out the recycling?" I asked.

"I'd love to." She responded without hesitating. I tilted my head with confusion. *Who was this girl? She's weird. She'd love to take out the recycling? Nobody says that.*

We turned the corner behind the supper club and I noticed a tire by the trash. When we lifted up the recycling lid, the empty cans looked familiar. This was all the trash from the beach, all the stuff I hung on Mooshy the Elk.

"Huh," I exclaimed.

"What?" Lily asked.

"It's nothing, nothing really I guess," I answered. "Did you put all this trash in here?"

"No," she responded innocently.

When I got back to Derek's table, he was gone. All his food was littered everywhere, his napkin on the floor.

Such a pig, I thought to myself. I can't even affect change on my own brother. Nobody noticed my Mooshy the Elk statement of rebellion, and so far I've made zero tips while waiting tables. That's when I noticed that Derek had left me three pennies and a note that read, "You suck as a waitress."

I biked out to Echo Point, the only place where I was able to get good cell reception, and texted Brooke.

"Brooke, I need you. I'm on the edge of the cliff and I've made no impact on this little island."

She wrote back right away, "Hang in there, kitten! You

just got there. I wish I was there with you!"

I stared down at my phone, wanting more. I wanted her beside me, but she was hours away. Brooke's innocent looks and sweet nature balanced out my temper and impatience, I felt unbalanced without my sidekick.

I looked out onto the gigantic lake and focused on something. It was a person with red hair and pale shoulders. Was it Lily? I had just seen her, so probably not. This person swam fast to shore. I moved in a little closer and noticed it was a boy; he looked like he might be around my age.

I know what you're thinking, but I wasn't interested in him in the least. He didn't even move me into the "lust" phase of love. I mean, this guy wore nerdy floral Hawaiian shorts. Who wears those anymore? Could he have been the guy who waterskied without the skis? The guy who looked deep into my eyes for a split second? I wasn't sure, but I did notice the following:

He was so pale that he almost glowed.

And he was fit.

Like, really fit.

Swim team fit.

Model fit.

Okay, he looked like a model.

Maybe he only looked like a model from far away. If I got closer, would he turn into a troll? He stood in the sand as I watched him. The waves swept up around his feet and he stared toward the horizon.

I thought he looked back and saw me, but I wasn't sure. A few rain drops fell, so I looked up to the sky. When I looked back down, I didn't see a trace of him.

The rain fell harder, so I raced off on my bike. It didn't

bother me that it was raining and that I was getting soaked. I didn't have anywhere I needed to be and the rain felt nice in the July heat.

I biked and biked and finally coasted down a long curving hill. In less than a second, I lost complete control.

I had that this-is-going-to-hurt-really-bad feeling. I closed my eyes and expected to be banged and scraped up. I pictured myself somersaulting through the rough gravel and winding up with a hundred cuts and scratches.

But the next thing I knew, I was floating through the air in a kind of slow motion. I wasn't really sure what had happened. It didn't seem real. Did I hit my head and dream it all? I could have sworn that I didn't hit my head, though. I landed very slowly in the overgrown grass in the ditch, unharmed. *Uh, what just happened?*

I shook my head in disbelief and looked around for a witness. Nobody seemed to be around, so I made it to my feet and brushed the hair off my face. I stood in shock for a moment, not knowing what to do, but feeling so lucky for not having a scratch on me.

I didn't want to stay long because the rain was turning into a real thunderstorm. I hopped back on my bike and thought I saw the Hawaiian-shorts guy running through the field. I did a double-take, but there was nobody there.

I decided it was best not to tell anyone about what happened. I had already held a snowflake in July and seen a water-skier who might not have really been there.

This should have been the end to my evening, but I had a hard time sleeping. I was thinking about my mysterious bike crash where I managed not to get a scrape on me. There seemed to be no answer to that mystery, so I focused on my bigger goal of making a statement against garbage and pollution that went completely unnoticed.

I'm sure you can guess where I wound up at three in the morning. Yep, I had a date with Mooshy the gigantic elk statue. The storm had passed and I brought him three trash bags of bottles, car parts, and other junk I found along a different beach. I fused it all together with some rope that had washed up and made a mad spider web of trash. A gross spectacle of consumer waste. I stood back to marvel at the madness I had just created.

"You again."

A scratchy young voice came from the woods. I turned, shocked, but not scared. I was secretly a little excited to have a witness to my statement, since it didn't work the night before. I looked around, but saw nobody.

"Hello . . . ?" I asked.

"Good morning," said the mystery voice. I spun around, but couldn't locate the voice's source.

I asked, "Good morning, or good night. Who's there?"

"It's morning right now, Theresa."

"What? How do you know my name?"

I noticed that clean lake fragrance again. I remembered it from last night.

"I'm going to call the police." I held up my phone.

I heard nothing for a few long moments. "Up here, Theresa. I don't want you to be scared. I'm sorry," the voice said.

I looked up and he suddenly materialized, sitting atop Mooshy. The guy with the red hair and old-fashioned Hawaiian shorts. He was wearing those shorts and no shirt.

"Uh, how do you know my name?"

"My sister told me about you."

"Are you Lily's brother?"

"Yep."

He slid effortlessly down the statue and shook my hand. I blushed a little, being so close to him without his shirt on.

"My name is Max," he said politely.

"I'm Theresa, but I guess you already know that. Uh, why aren't you wearing any clothes?"

"Why are you up so late?" he replied with a question.

I let go of his hand.

"I mean your shirt. Where's your shirt?" I asked. He walked around Mooshy, studying him.

"What are you doing to poor Mooshy?" This guy, he thinks he's so cute by answering my questions with his own questions.

"Will you answer my question?"

"Will you answer mine?" he said with a smile.

Okay, this was getting annoying. I didn't have time for this. I had to get to bed. I picked up my bike and hopped on the seat, but something felt different. I had a flat tire.

"Just great!"

"What?" Max asked.

"I have to walk home, my tire is flat." I started to lock up my bike on a sign post.

"Could I accompany you home?" Max asked.

"No, that's okay. It's really not that far."

"Come on. I'm not exactly a stranger, you know my sister. And I want to hear what you have against Mooshy."

"Nothing. I only have a beef with the humans who didn't recycle all this trash," I explained.

"Why don't you recycle it yourself?"

"Because I want people to notice what they were doing to the island. Then I will recycle it."

Max looked at me for a long time. A small smile came across his face. He said nothing and I got uncomfortable with the silence.

"What?" I asked.

"What?" he answered. Just to be annoying, I'm sure of it. He continued his intense stare.

"Did you get those shorts from your grandpa?" I asked to be sorta mean and break the silence. They were not the shorts of your average teenager.

"Yep. This swimsuit once belonged to my grandfather Thomas. He says they're vintage. He collects them."

Didn't he know that I was being sarcastic? I did not understand this guy Max at all. Who wears grandpa swimsuits? Was he joking? Who knows? His Hawaiian shorts reminded me of something, though.

"Were you barefoot waterskiing the other day?" I asked.

"What's that?"

"Waterskiing without the water skis."

"I've never been on water skis, have you?" he replied.

"I could have sworn that it was you."

"Are you sure it was me?"

"Red hair, pale skin. And I thought you maybe saw me, too."

"Hmmmm," was all he said. I didn't have the patience to find out the real story.

"I'm leaving," I said, annoyed.

"I have a confession," he said to get me to stay. "If I tell you, will you let me walk you home?" This question caused me to raise a suspicious eyebrow.

"What is it?" I asked.

"I was the one who cleaned up Mooshy last night," he

admitted. "I didn't know what your intentions were. Now that I do, I'll wait a day to clean him up."

I was furious that he had ruined my statement. "I can clean him up myself tomorrow night. That was my plan the whole time."

I stormed off, but he caught up. He walked backwards in front of me and apologized.

"I'm sorry, I really am. I believe in your statement." I slowed down to a stop and took a deep breath. *Maybe I should give him a chance.* I exhaled, a little too dramatically.

"Do you know of any shortcuts back to my Aunt Kat's?" I asked.

"Do you like an adventure?"

"Would you not answer my question with a question?"

"Is that what you want me to do?"

I gave him my best "I'm going to melt you with the laser rays coming from my eyeballs" look, to which he responded with a simple, "Follow me."

I followed Max down a trail that led close to the water's edge. We hiked along the large rocks toward Aunt Kat's house.

Did I have a crush on Max? He pretty much looked like a model. He was fit as a swimmer, but I don't think I did. So . . . there.

I was just trying to figure him out, mostly looking at his back and shoulders. He was as pale as Lily, pretty built, and had cool freckles on his cheeks and shoulders.

I admit it, I was checking him out, but how could I not? He was marching away, right in front of me. For the first time that night, I noticed that he wasn't wearing any shoes. He seemed like the ultimate beach bum, but he didn't have a

California surfer accent and he seemed to talk smartly and deliberately.

Who was this guy?

He was as weird as his sister Lily. Were their parents, like, massive hippies or something? Did he grow up in the trees with Tarzan?

I followed him along the trail; he kept looking back at me to make sure I was doing okay. The sun started to peek out and at that moment, he looked back at me again. A line of sun flared around his deep hazel eyes. I couldn't focus because the sun was right behind him. It was like the ultimate Instagram filter. A filter they wish they had designed. I had the sudden urge to whip out my phone and capture the moment. I needed to study him more. How could he have such a pale face, but such glowing cheeks? Perhaps it happens a lot, but it's nothing I'd ever seen before. I must have involuntarily stopped walking because out of nowhere, he grasped my hand.

"Are you okay?" he asked softly. It took me a second to take it all in. He had such a calm tone in his voice.

"I'm good," I said. He let go of my hand as he pointed across the woods.

"There it is. Your aunt's place."

"Thanks for taking me this far."

"My pleasure," he said. I scrunched up my face at his old-fashioned politeness.

"Why are you so old fashioned?" I asked.

"What brings you to that conclusion?"

"Because you just are." He started hiking toward town backwards, facing me.

"I enjoyed our time together, Theresa."

I waved off his last statement and turned toward Aunt

Kat's home, rolling my eyes. I took a few steps and looked back to see what he was doing, but he was no longer on the trail. He had pretty much . . . vanished.

I snuck into the house and crept upstairs to the attic. I figured I would sleep for a couple of hours. The sun came through the attic window, so I started to close the curtains. I got them almost closed, but then changed my mind. I opened them back up and opened the window too. A gust of wind came through the screen. I took in a deep breath; I still sensed the fragrance of the fresh lake.

Was Max someone I had "the hots" for? Did I find him attractive right away? Within the first ninety seconds? Science says it only takes ninety seconds. I knew that I liked his voice and that he was unlike anyone I'd ever met. He seemed to appear and disappear. I felt like I had known him for a long time. I felt safe with him. I took a deep breath and watched the horizon for any sign of Max, but there was none.

"I enjoyed our time together, Theresa." I repeated Max's line to myself as my head hit the pillow. I wasn't able to fall asleep, so I grabbed my laptop and did a search for Max.

I looked in every corner of the internet, but I didn't come up with much of anything. It figures that Max wouldn't be on social media; he seemed too private and weird for that. When I searched for "Max" and "Echo Island," all I came up with was a realtor from the mainland named Max who was in his sixties. I gave up on my cyber investigation and closed my eyes.

Even though it was summer, the night turned chilly and I had to rub my feet together to warm them up. I love using a thick blanket on a cool summer night. A rare occurrence in July, but up north things are different. Now that I had met Max, things were really different.

Monday, July 11th

In the morning, I walked to work with a lot nervous energy. I knew this time that my statement against littering was going to last through the morning. I was also nervous because I was running late for my shift at the supper club. I'd have to check out Mooshy after work.

I guess that's what I get for staying out late and making political statements with one of the weirdest guys on the planet: Max, the half-naked local who wears his grandpa's Hawaiian swimsuits.

I didn't have to be near Mooshy to hear of my impact—I found out from people at the restaurant.

"Why would someone have something against Mooshy?"

"Some drunks probably did it."

"Did anyone call the police?"

These were all statements I overheard at the supper club as I ran around, taking orders and refilling coffee. What was I expecting? People to reevaluate their whole lives? Become instant activists for the environment? Contemplate their consumer choices? Make them feel guilty about not reusing or recycling? Sort of, I guess. I don't know. Either way, my goal to bring attention to the litter failed again. Everyone wanted someone to blame.

Maybe I should have hung a sign around Mooshy's neck that read, "Please Recycle," or something like that. What would Brooke do? I didn't have time to bike up to Echo Point and text her.

Then the thought hit me: how am I going to clean it all up tonight? I could get in serious trouble if someone found out I had done it. More than one person mentioned calling the police. I came up with an idea and presented it to Aunt Kat.

"I'd like to volunteer to clean up Mooshy," I said.

"That's so sweet of you. Do you need any help?" she asked.

"I think I got it. I'd like to recycle all that I can. How does that sound?" I added.

"There's too much to haul back here, but there's a recycling drop-off at the clearing on the way to Echo Point. Use my bike trailer if you'd like."

"Perfect," I said.

My shift was finally almost over when I noticed something odd. I saw Lily with a cut finger. I swear I saw blood as she held her finger with her other hand. She didn't panic or anything; she slowly put her finger under the running water and closed her eyes. She didn't realize I was watching. When she took her finger out, there was no blood or cut or anything. Maybe it was ketchup or something else, but I could've sworn it was blood.

"Did you cut yourself?" I asked.

"Oh, I'm okay," she answered calmly.

"Isn't there blood on your finger?"

"Everything is okay. Take a look for yourself."

Lily showed me her finger and she was right—there wasn't even a trace of a cut. I shook my head and laughed at myself.

"Hmmm, I must be seeing things." Lily didn't respond. She stared into my eyes the way Max had. Those eyes that looked wise beyond her years. She gave me the tiniest smile and it felt like time had stopped. I got lost in her eyes almost as bad as I had been lost in Max's eyes. I finally snapped out of it.

"Sure you're okay?"

She smiled and said, "Yes."

I'm not a hugger, but I felt like I wanted to protect Lily from something, so I gave her a quick hug. She hugged me back and she was so warm and welcoming. Since I'm a nerd, I had studied the act of hugging. When we embrace, our bodies reduce the amount of the stress hormone, cortisol. Hugs also release tension and send calming messages to the brain. It's funny to say, but Lily was really good at hugging. Some people aren't. It's something I've noticed in my wise old age of fifteen.

I finished my shift and hiked back to Mooshy to fix the flat tire and clean up. It seemed like everyone from town had seen Mooshy and had moved on with their day. I noticed far off in the distance that the ferry was about to dock. That would mean a whole new crop of tourists from the mainland. I didn't want to deal with all the wrong interpretations of my Mooshy statement over and over, so I cleaned him up in record time.

I kept thinking about Max. Would he stop by and see what people thought? I'd look over my shoulder now and again, expecting him to be there with some random old-fashioned polite question, but he never showed up.

I raced off on the bike and made my way toward Echo Point with all the empty cans and bottles in the bike trailer. Halfway there, I came upon a hybrid car and a middle-aged man wandering around looking at his cell phone. *He must not know the secret place to get a good signal*, I thought to myself. This guy looked nice enough, kind of outdoorsy, with a beard. He had a fleece jacket similar to the one I had; he seemed harmless.

"Are you lost?" I offered. "Or do you need a stronger signal?"

"A little bit of both. Do you live on the island?" he asked.

"No, but if you keep going to Echo Point, you'll get a strong enough signal to make a call."

"Where's Echo Point?"

"Another mile or so that way." I pointed east.

"Okay, great."

He approached me and shook my hand.

"Thank you. I'm George."

"I'm Theresa."

"Nice to meet you. You don't, uh, live on Echo?" he asked.

"Nope, I'm only here for a week and a half or so."

"What's with the bike trailer?"

"Just taking these cans to the recycling drop-off."

"We need more young people like you," he said with a smile. "What's up with that fork?" he asked. Not many people notice or care to ask about my fork necklace/revolution statement, but I was flattered that he did.

"Oh, it's nothing. It's a reusable fork I take with me, so I can reduce waste," I said.

"Wow, good for you!" he said earnestly. "Imagine if everyone wore those, we wouldn't need to make any plastic forks ever again."

I was floored; somebody actually got my fork's potential to start a revolution, one small step at a time!

"They're easy to make," I said. "I found a fork I liked and drilled a hole into it at my school's industrial arts shop."

"Very industrious," he said with a smile.

I'm used to a select few adults who compliment Brooke and me on our goals for the planet. But usually, adults are super annoyed with the stuff we do. I got uncomfortable with the attention from George, so I focused back on him.

"Looks like important work," I said.

He replied with a smile, "Yeah. I'm monitoring a project up here. I'm sort of an environmental consultant," he answered.

"What for?" I asked.

"Oh, monitoring the lake's pollution levels," he said.

I had heard of a fracking project on Echo Island, but Aunt Kat and a bunch of the locals had it shut down. Brooke and I studied fracking after we learned about the protest.

Fracking is short for hydraulic fracturing. To do it, they have to inject a massive amount of chemicals into the ground, which allows the release of gas. It's very difficult to recover and dispose of the chemicals once they're in the ground, though. Was this George guy part of the fracking company? As one of the founding members of Earth's Last Chance Club, I pushed the subject.

"The fracking project?" I asked.

He smiled a little before responding, "You know about that?"

"Yeah, my aunt and her friends fought that and won. They didn't want 596 toxic chemicals being shot underneath the ground, near her house."

He raised both his eyebrows at that one.

"Wow, you've really studied your fracking," he exclaimed.

"I've done some research. It's really scary. Flammable drinking water, man-made earthquakes, animals losing their hair. I know it's very hard to clean up and could destroy this island."

"I agree," he said.

But I was on a roll, fueled by anger. "They leave the chemicals out in ponds to evaporate in the sun, but you can't ever get rid of the toxic chemicals. They evaporate and just rain back down on us like poison. I mean, would you drink water from this lake if 596 chemicals were spilled in it?"

He was about to respond when two sort of gnarly looking guys showed up. Like, how gnarly? They had bad teeth and lots of tattoos on their knuckles. It wasn't so much how they looked, but how they acted. They wouldn't make eye contact with me.

"We didn't get the invite to the party," one of them said.

Hello, creep factor on high alert. George's face turned bright red, he seemed ashamed to be with these two guys.

"Theresa, uh, this is Earl and Kyle. These fine brothers will be working with me," George said nervously. *Great, now they know my name,* I thought to myself.

Not sure how to respond to this, I said the usual, "It's nice to meet you."

"Yes it is," Earl said with a sleazy smile. Um, nasty. I might only be fifteen, but I can recognize a loser dude when I see one. I had to get out of there somehow. "I better get up to Echo Point," I said.

The detective in me wanted to stick around and get to the bottom of the story, but I sensed a weird danger. They were way too serious and way too nervous for your average meeting on a little picturesque island. I started to bike away, but I heard George yelling my name. I turned around and saw him running toward me. I stopped and he caught up to me. "You dropped your wallet," he said as he handed it out to me.

"Oh, crap. Thank you! I always do that. I sometimes forget to put it in my pocket all the way," I said.

"No purse for you, huh?" he joked.

"Nope, I'm not the handbag type," I said.

"Oh yeah, I guess people call them handbags, not purses," he said and laughed.

I didn't know what else to say, I was so relieved that he saw me drop it. "Thanks so much, I hate losing things." I looked over at the two brothers, Kyle and Earl. George must've noticed the look on my face.

"Oh, those guys. They're not so bad. A little weird, right?" he asked.

"A little."

"It's so beautiful up here, but there isn't much opportunity for the locals living here. You know? They're hard workers though."

"That's what's important," I offered. It was clear that George was a little embarrassed by these guys. Who was I to judge them? I was a city girl from an upper-middle-class family.

"Well, see you around the island. Thanks again for this," I said and held up my wallet.

"Of course. See you around."

I rode my bike to a grouping of trees and spied on them. I realize I said I shouldn't judge, but I was still too curious not to find out what would happen next.

The three talked for a little more, then George got in his car and drove off, but the two brothers wandered toward the cliff and looked out onto the lake.

I stashed my bike and followed Kyle and Earl, hiding behind some bushes. They moved right up to the edge of the cliff. I don't know how high it was from the water, but it looked pretty dangerous.

I snuck closer and made it behind a huge boulder. I was able to catch a little of what they were saying. Not full sentences, but I heard enough to understand that none of what they were saying was good.

"Dump the sludge."

"At night."

"Toxic."

"Nowhere else to hide it."

"We're gonna need more money."

Then it happened: my phone went off. An unmistakable sound. I took off immediately and ran along the cliff. I didn't dare look back, but I could feel them chasing me. I knew I wasn't supposed to discover what I had heard. My heart was beating so fast.

The adrenaline kicked in as I ran way too close to the edge of the cliff, but I had to continue on the trail because the gigantic lake was on one side and big rocks were on the other. I saw the woods ahead and I thought if I could just make it to the trees, I would lose them. I heard their steps and breathing getting closer and closer. I felt their hands on my shoulders and neck.

Then it all went black.

The next thing I remember: I was lying on a large, smooth rock surface in a small cave and I was soaking wet. I opened my eyes slowly, but then I quickly remembered the two men. I bolted upright, afraid and defensive, but there was only Max, also soaking wet. He hugged me tightly and whispered in my ear, "You're okay. You're okay."

My body ached pretty badly, but it was manageable. Max, like his sister, was really good at giving hugs. I was shaking, but he kept holding me until I finally said, "What happened?" I looked around the cave and noticed there was a pool of water, lit by a bunch of candles.

"You fell off the cliff. You might have been pushed," he explained.

"What?" was all I could muster.

"I was down on the beach, and I saw it," he said.

"I fell from the cliff? Shouldn't I be dead?" I asked, still not sure what had happened. I didn't let him respond. "Where are we? How did we get here?"

Max looked down at the ground, and then finally stood up.

I wiped the wet hair from my forehead and exhaled. "Why are we here?" I asked, desperate for at least one answer.

"I thought it would be safer here. Those guys, I think they wanted to harm you. So, I, uh . . . we swam here."

I couldn't really take it all in, but my first thought was: *This kind of thing doesn't happen down in the city.* I shook my head in disbelief. I looked at Max's hands. They were shaking. "Thank you for getting me here," I said.

He noticed me staring at his hands. He shook off his nervousness and looked at me with another long, serious stare that he and his sister were really *really* good at. It's usually impolite to stare that long at someone, but it didn't feel that way with Max.

"Thank you," I said again with a whisper.

"Of course," he replied softly. He offered a tiny smile. He

paced around the cave slowly. "We have to get you out of here somehow," he finally said.

"Can't we climb out?" I asked.

"We're, uh, fifty feet underwater," he admitted. He gave me yet another long stare; he looked so serious. So not like any teenager I've ever met.

"We're underwater?" I asked. "Why are we here? How did we get here?"

"Those guys. I've seen them before. Heard what they've said before. They want to destroy the lake," he said seriously.

"Are they with the fracking company?" I asked. He tilted his head, unsure what to say next.

"I'm sorry, I don't know what fracking is," he said in a shy way.

"It's hundreds of toxic chemicals they inject into the earth to free up oil or natural gas."

"That doesn't sound good," he said.

"They try to clean them up afterwards, but it usually doesn't work. It pollutes the groundwater because they usually can't retrieve much of the chemicals once they've injected them."

He looked at me and then looked down at his hands. He seemed so sad. "We've already noticed a change in the lake. It's not as clean as it used to be," he offered. "I think those guys want to make it worse."

"I know they do," I said and added, "They said something about dumping sludge. Maybe those are the chemicals left over from fracking somewhere else. My aunt helped to stop it on the island, but they must be doing it nearby or they still have the chemicals or something. From what I overheard, I bet they want to dump it near the island."

"What can we do?" he asked.

"We can try to stop them," I said as I stood up. I stumbled a little. I suddenly felt a little dizzy.

"We're running out of oxygen. We have to get you to the surface," he said.

"What if those guys are still out there?" I asked, breathing heavily.

"I can get you to a secret beach. They won't see us." Max grabbed my hand and escorted me to the water. "If you start to panic, like you're running out of air, just tap my shoulder. Okay?"

"Then what will you do?" I asked.

"I'll get you some air. It's a really long swim and we have to stay below the surface," he responded.

"Wait. How is that going to work?"

He smiled at me and then said, "You have to trust me. I can swim underwater for a long time," he said.

"But I can't," I protested.

"You'll get to the surface." I thought about asking more questions, but something made me trust him. I don't know what it was, but when I looked him in the eye, I somehow knew we'd be okay, even if it defied logic.

He squeezed my hand and we climbed into the water. I didn't really have another option. We were running out of air.

We were up to our necks when we took our last big breath and went underwater. We swam fast and hard, but it was taking forever. I started to panic, but I kept swimming and swimming.

Then real panic set in. Like, really bad panic. I tapped Max on the shoulder, but then he seemed to have disappeared.

This next part is hard to accept. I wouldn't believe it myself, but it *did* happen. Even as I write, I'm still not sure what had occurred, because it happened so fast.

Suddenly it felt like I was coming to the surface of the water, because my head was out of the water and I was able to breathe. I was swimming underwater, but breathing air inside some sort of unfathomable bubble.

I looked around and saw the real surface of the water far above me. It seemed like I had a foot of air above my head that allowed me to breathe when I was almost out of breath. Like I said, very, very hard to accept. I took a couple deep breaths and the bubble disappeared.

I saw Max swimming below me, but then I couldn't spot him anymore. Did he cause the bubble? I didn't have a good explanation for what had happened, but there must've been one.

I wasn't panicking anymore and before long, I broke the surface. Safe, but gasping for air. Max reappeared and we swam quickly to the shore. We snuck low to the ground and sat down behind a huge boulder.

"What was that?" I asked Max, still catching my breath.

"What was what?" he asked.

"That bubble of air," I answered.

"I'm not sure," he said. "Air bubbles happen in this lake. They sometimes cling to people."

"Did you do that?"

"Did I do what?" he asked.

"Make an air bubble so I could breathe?"

"How would I do that?"

"I, uh . . . I don't know," I said, confused.

Max grabbed my hand in a hurry. "I think I hear someone, we have to go," he said. We snuck off the small beach and moved south along the water. We climbed between the rocks, up a cliff trail, and darted into the woods.

Max took my hand and we ran like crazy. I kept looking behind me for any sign of Kyle or Earl or whatever their names were, but I didn't notice anyone behind us.

"Can we stop?" I asked, out of breath. Max didn't slow down, but he turned and said seriously, "We're almost there." We ran and ran and arrived at a small clearing with a creek. We caught our breath and eventually sat on some rocks. We squeezed some of the water out of our clothes.

"What are we going to do now?" I asked.

"Were you on your bike?" he asked. Max answered questions with questions, even in a crisis.

"I was. I had the trailer full of cans and bottles," I answered.

"Let's leave it there until tomorrow. I don't want to risk seeing those guys again."

"Do you know them?" I asked.

"I've seen them on the remote parts of the island, but not very often. They live on the mainland, around Kingfield."

"What if they find me again, or come into the supper club?" I asked.

"We'll have to get you a disguise or something," he offered.

"Like what?" I asked.

"I'm not sure yet," he replied. "We're going to have to change your appearance, though."

The next thing I knew, it was dark out and Max and I were in the gas station bathroom with a box of hair bleach from the corner store. I locked the door nervously.

"This will turn your hair blond?" he asked.

"It's supposed to," I answered.

"How does that work?" he asked.

"Crap. It's a bunch of chemicals. Should we return it? I wasn't thinking," I said. Max tried to read the box, but his face scrunched up in confusion.

"This probably shouldn't go down the drain. A lot of the water used on the island goes back into the lake," he said.

I had to worry about my safety and going blond was now part of that. I turned the box over and read the ingredients out loud: "Hydrogen peroxide, phosphoric acid, etidronic acid, cetylstearylalcohol, ceteareth-25, sodium laury sulfate, acrylates copolymer, methacrylate copolymer, and dimethicone."

Um, I'm sure none of this was good for any human or animal or fish or blade of grass. This blond hair idea was starting to sound really stupid.

Couldn't I get a pair of fake glasses? Wear a hat or cut my hair? I looked up at Max and he had the saddest look on his face. He swallowed a lump in his throat and stared at me with that now-famous-to-me intense stare.

"We're going to do something else," I stated.

"But how will you hide?" he asked.

"I'm only here for a short time; there's a lot I can do."

I opened the bathroom door with determination and marched back over to the corner store to return the bleaching kit.

"Is there anything wrong with this purchase?" the cashier asked.

I answered, "I'm not going to participate in poisoning the planet, you, your children, or your grandchildren."

I felt pretty proud of that statement. The cashier's expression went blank and he said nothing for a moment before he offered, "Here's your two-seventy-nine back."

I spotted sunglasses and a baseball hat and thought they might work as a good disguise. It was better than nothing, so I bought them instead.

I left the store and I saw Max looking in the window of the Tavern restaurant, staring at the fish aquarium. The fish were going to be dinner for tomorrow's customers.

This wasn't normal window shopping. I had to remember, this was Max. Things were different with him. The street was empty and a single street light illuminated the scene. He reached out with his finger and touched the window. All the fish swam toward it. He looked so focused that I didn't want to interrupt him. He heard my steps, though, and looked up.

"Oh, hi. How did it go?" he asked.

"They took it back, but he didn't care about my statement against the hair industry," I answered.

"I'm worried about you," he said.

I replied with confidence, "I'll be fine, plus I got these."

I showed him the glasses and hat. Max gave me a small smile, but I knew that he was still worried. We both heard the sound of a loud truck coming toward us from a few blocks away. Max looked at me, concerned.

"We better hide," I said.

"Just in case," he agreed. We darted into an alley and waited to see who it was.

Good thing we did, because it was the dirty truck that belonged to those scary brothers. My eyes widened and I looked to Max as we watched Kyle and Earl hop out.

Max's mouth dropped open in shock, but I covered it with my hand. I understood he wasn't going to say anything, but I was so scared, I didn't even want him breathing.

Kyle finished his beer and threw the can on the ground.

His brother, Earl, finished his and crushed it beneath his boot. They ran into the corner store and we debated what to do.

"Let's run," Max whispered, but I disagreed.

"I think we should stay here. They'd never expect us here." Max took a deep breath, but nodded his head in agreement. The brothers came out of the store, lighting cigarettes and talking. They leaned up against their truck to smoke.

Kyle ripped one of Aunt Kat's Blue Moon Dance posters off a telephone pole and said, "Great, that stupid dance is this Friday."

Earl responded, "So what?"

"That's the night we're going to dump that sludge over here," Kyle whispered angrily.

"Big deal."

"The big deal is"—Kyle was on a roll—"we've got ten barrels of that crap to dump. Somebody's gonna see us."

Max squinted his eyes in anger at the two men. I did, too. I gripped his hand. It felt way too early to hold Max's hand. I mean, I wasn't even interested in him, not really. It seemed like the right thing to do though. I could barely breathe, my mouth was so dry. We continued to listen.

Earl grabbed the poster from Kyle's hand, studied it, and said, "You idiot, this dance is on the mainland, in Kingfield. We'll be over here by Echo Point. The whole damn town goes to that dance. Nobody will be on the island to see us."

"Okay, we'll stick to our plan. Let's get on that ferry. This island, man. So boring. The bars are already closed," Kyle said. Then he crumpled up the poster and lit it on fire with his cigarette. It ignited into a small ball of flames and floated silently to the ground. He stomped on it and dropped his cigarette. They jumped in the truck and took off.

When they were a few blocks away, Max looked to me and said, "We won't have to worry about them finding you, at least. They'll be in Kingfield."

"Yeah, not tonight and not on the island, at least for a while," I responded. "I don't understand. Why would they pollute the lake?" he asked.

"They're doing it for money. And those chemicals would kill thousands of animals for years and years."

Max looked terrified. "What do we do now?" he asked. "We're going to stop them," I answered.

Max walked me home and we left my bike where it was for the time being. Neither one of us could think straight about what to do, but we knew that it was safest to get me home. He gave me a big hug and whispered in my ear, "We'll figure out what to do tomorrow. But we will stop them. Okay?"

"Okay. Thanks for walking me home," I said.

"Of course," he replied.

I stood at the end of Aunt Kat's drive and watched him turn the corner on the street. I was ready to go in, but I thought of something. What did I really know of Max? Basically next to nothing. I knew that Lily was his sister and that he lived with his grandfather, Thomas. I knew that he was super odd, but interesting. Super fit with red hair, but what else?

It wasn't that late, so I followed him. I don't know why, I guess I wanted more information about him. He plodded along slowly, so he was easy to follow. He never once looked back and I have to say, it was so awesome to play detective.

He roamed past the restaurant again and tapped on the window. The fish swam toward his hand again. He just stared at them, and looked to the ground and exhaled. A fish jumped in the air and Max laughed a little to himself. I saw some ash floating through the air and Max looked up; he noticed it as well. Was it really ash or was it snow? Was I totally seeing things, thinking it would be snowing again in July? A strong wind blew all the snow or ash away, so I wasn't able to determine what it truly was.

He wandered again and I followed. Before long, he was at the Echo Oasis, his grandfather Thomas's bar. I hid behind a tree and watched him go into Thomas's home. The house was really cool. It was covered in wood shingles and had plants and little trees everywhere. Thomas had antique signs hanging all over the house, too. You could tell that someone interesting lived there.

Thomas turned out the lights and locked up the bar. Lily and Max emerged from the house and gave him a hug. Then the oddest thing happened. It was like they were saying goodbye. Max and Lily hiked off into the woods and Thomas went inside. Were they sleeping in a tent somewhere?

I snuck through the woods to follow, but I couldn't catch up. I saw them in the moonlight, but quickly lost track of the two. I stumbled upon a trail and followed it. It led to a rocky beach. Were they going to take a swim? Roast marshmallows over a fire on the beach? But when I got to the beach, there was nothing. I looked up to the moon and noticed that it was almost full. There were only four more days before the Blue Moon Dance. A night that promised fun, but possible danger for me and catastrophe for the lake. Either way, I had to come up with a plan.

Tuesday, July 12th

I was distracted by the previous night's events all morning long. I had to wait tables at Kat's, but I did nothing but make mistakes. I wore my baseball hat disguise and looked over my shoulder constantly. Aunt Kat pulled me aside and asked if I was feeling well. I was physically, but not mentally or emotionally or whatever.

"Well, you let me know if you need a break or anything, okay?" she offered. I kept thinking of Max's face and how stressed out he was. I focused back to my tables, and that's when I spilled coffee on my brother's table.

"Nice going, space cadet," he complained.

"Whatever, I'm sorry. Is that what you want to hear?" I replied.

"I want my coffee in my cup and not all over Aunt Kat's paperwork. Not that much to ask."

"Did I ruin any of her papers?" I asked.

"It's fine. Just ... What's wrong with you?" he said, annoyed.

"I've got bigger things on my mind. Things that would poison your water and poison your coffee. Things like fracking."

"Don't you know that fracking and mining create jobs and get us energy?" he asked.

"Okay, so you won't mind if your drinking water is flammable?" I asked.

"There's no proof of that," he said as he handed me his finished plates. "Take these away. I'm done."

"You are such a loser," I said in a loud whisper.

"Nice hat. Since when did you like baseball?"

A few customers were starting to witness our little brother/sister spat, so I took off to the kitchen. Lily was doing dishes and she noticed how stressed I was.

"Everything okay?" she asked.

"It's my brother. He's turning into my parents about twenty years before I thought he would. Don't you want to strangle your brother sometimes?" I asked.

"We usually get along," she replied. I forgot that I was talking to Lily, who was talking about Max. Those two weren't your average brother and sister. I wanted to ask her where she went the night before, but then I'd have to admit that I had spied on them. Suddenly, Lily turned to me and gripped my arm.

"Max found something out. He needs to talk to you as soon as you can get away," she said.

"Where can I find him?"

"He's waiting for you at the end of our trail," she answered.

"Which trail?"

"An ancient trail behind Grandpa Thomas's bar," she said. "You can find it behind our home. Do you know where the Echo Oasis is?"

I pretended not to know what she was talking about, but I instantly thought of the trail from the previous night—the one I was on while trying to follow her and Max.

"I'm sure I'll be able to find it," I offered.

Lily added, "If you touch the northeast corner of our house and then walk one hundred steps toward the lake, you'll be at the beginning of the trail. I'd take you there, but I have to work through lunch."

"Not a problem," I said. Lily took the apron from my hands and shuffled me out of the kitchen. "He's waiting, please hurry."

I arrived at their house and snuck to the corner. Behind the house, I noticed my bike and trailer. Max must have gotten it for me.

I was still kind of scared to be tramping around the island or waiting tables, but I felt safe knowing those guys were barely ever on the island.

I glimpsed up at his grandfather's bar and saw Thomas whistling and doing dishes. Out of nowhere, I heard a branch break. I spun around and realized it was just a baby deer. We had a miniature staring contest because neither one of us knew what to do. I took a couple slow steps toward her, and she didn't run. I moved in for a third step, but the deer took off, her little white tail bouncing in the dark woods.

I made my way down the trail and before long, I could hear the waves of the lake hitting the shore. I kept going until I came across a piece of birch bark tied to a tree. I took it down and discovered it was a note.

It read, "You're almost there. —Max." I tucked it into my pocket and smiled. Once again, I had to ask myself, who was this guy? I was now determined to find out.

I made it out of the woods and onto the small rocky beach. Max was standing there, staring out onto the lake. He turned his face to mine and it sort of took my breath away.

He looked different; there was something more serious about him. He had a look of urgency not found often in my high school back in the city. This was no minor text messaging issue. No minor, "I'm not getting a wi-fi signal" issue. No, "We're out of frozen pizza" issue. He saw me and started to push his canoe into the water.

"We don't have much time to waste," was all he said. I helped him launch the canoe and we both jumped in.

"What's happening?" I asked.

"I'll tell you once we get away from the beach," he replied. We both paddled pretty hard for a while, but then I noticed that it got easier, the wind was at our backs, helping us coast toward the mainland.

"Let's take a break," he said. I was sitting in front, so I turned around to face him. He kept paddling.

"I thought we were taking a break?" I complained.

"We are, but I still need to steer a little. Don't worry," he said. I looked down and noticed a big rolled-up plaid blanket.

"Feel free to use the blanket to sleep on if you'd like," he offered.

"Um, it's summer, so I don't need a blanket," I said.

"Don't you work early mornings?" he asked.

"Today I did," I replied.

"Then you must be tired. Right?"

"A little, but not really," I said. He smiled his polite, serene smile that he was so good at, but I wasn't having it. I wasn't going to nap, even though I was tired.

"Why are we going to the mainland?" I asked.

"I heard those guys last night while I was over in Kingfield," he said.

"What were they talking about?"

"Something about meeting over lunch today to talk about the chemicals."

"Oh. Really? Doesn't sound good. Where are they meeting?" I asked.

"Behind the old gazebo," he replied.

"What else did they say?" I asked.

"That was it. They talked about the dance again and I know that's in a few days, so I knew we didn't have a lot of time," he replied. "I don't want them to recognize you, so I borrowed these from Lily." He handed me a bag and I looked at it with suspicion. I opened it up and pulled out a blue wig and some thick-rimmed glasses.

"Excuse me?" I managed to say with shock.

"Your disguise. I don't want them to know it's you," he said. "Try it on." I didn't want him to know, but I secretly had always wanted blue hair.

"Do I have to right now?" I asked.

"I think you should wear it on the mainland, to be safe."

"It's better than the disguise I bought the other night."

I tried it on and shook it out a little. I felt shy all of a sudden and looked to him for approval.

"What do you think? Is it me?" I asked.

"It's you and it isn't at the same time. If you put on Lily's glasses, nobody would guess it was you," he said.

I put on the glasses and pretended to be more inquisitive. I thought, *Now is the time to ask him some hard-hitting reporter-type questions*. I had my glasses on and all.

"So, Max," I started.

"Yes?"

"Where do you go to school?" I asked.

"It's on the mainland, you wouldn't know it."

"I could look it up on my phone?"

"I don't think so. Your phone won't work in the middle of the lake. I can assure you."

I looked at my phone and he was right, no bars. Dang it.

"Okay, how old are you?" I continued, unfazed.

"How old are you?" he responded. I knew it! I knew he'd respond with a question.

"I'm fifteen," I answered. "You?"

"I'm sixteen," he replied.

I pushed my glasses closer to my face and pretended to write his answers down.

"How long does it take to canoe to the mainland?"

"Are you in a hurry?" he asked.

"Well, sort of. You were so urgent before," I answered.

"Now that we're on our way, we can only go so fast," he countered. I guess that was true. But what was also true was that I had time to grill him like a news reporter.

"Do you have any other siblings?" I asked.

"It's just Lily and me," he answered.

"Where are your parents?" I blurted out without even thinking.

"They're no longer with us," he answered.

Ooops.

I was silent for a moment. He was as young as me, so I didn't even think of his parents being gone as an option. Everyone I know who is around my age, they still have their parents around. Youngish and active and healthy.

"I'm sorry," I finally said. "I should've been more sensitive with my questions."

"It's okay. Really. I don't mind. I enjoy talking about them, remembering them." This was too honest of an answer; I wasn't ready for something like that. I started to get uncomfortable. I wanted to change the subject really bad.

He must have sensed what I was thinking, so he started talking. "Those feelings you're having don't have to be awkward or embarrassing. If you feel strange right now, it shows that you're a sensitive person. And that sensitivity is your true wealth. Your power. You should be proud of it because not everyone has it. In reality, very few people do," he said.

Was he trying to make me faint? Nobody *ever* said anything like that to me before. How could a teenage beach bum wind up talking like a wise old man?

Okay, so we were talking about me and talking about our feelings. Now was the real time to change the subject! Yeeeesh. I don't like to get personal, yuck!

"What's your favorite subject in school?" I asked while imagining my palm hitting my forehead. What a bad way to change the subject. The look on Max's face? He knew exactly what I was trying to do.

"I like all the subjects. How about you?" he answered.

"Sorry, that was a lame question," I said. "I know what Lily does, but what's your job?"

"I work at my grandfather's bar. Restocking beer and cleaning up," he said.

I thought about the night that I followed Max to his home. The night that he and Lily walked off and suddenly I blurted out, "Do you have another house or do you stay at your grandfather's place?"

"Why do you ask that?" he asked.

I lied, "It seems like it might be too small for you and Lily and your grandfather." Max looked back at me with a more serious expression. "We all live there together. We make do with the size."

"Got it," I said. I nodded my head.

I was done with the twenty questions for now. I had gone too far and felt uncomfortable. I nervously played with my fork necklace. Max didn't seem angry by my last question, but I felt like I had pried too much.

"I like your necklace," Max said.

"Thanks."

"I wish more people would do that. Everyone seems like they want to use something once and then throw it in the lake the second they are done with it."

"That's why I wear this."

"I figured that might be the reason," he said and stared deep into my eyes. I almost blurted out, *You can stop staring at me at any point now, it's making me uncomfortable*, but I didn't. There was just too much face-to-face talking going on, but I remembered his suggestion from earlier.

"You know, I got up so early, I think I'll take a nap like you suggested. Is that okay?" I asked.

"Of course. Make yourself comfortable," he said, "and here's a pillow for you if you'd like it." He handed me a pad from underneath his seat. I made a little bed with the huge blanket and pad and listened to the waves. The water made the best white noise and I managed to doze off for a little bit.

I woke up to a scraping sound and quickly realized that it was the bottom of the canoe scraping the sand—we had hit the beach on the mainland. Max handed me Lily's glasses and said, "Don't forget these." I rubbed my eyes, straightened my blue wig, and did my best to wake up.

"Do you make it over here to Kingfield a lot?" I asked.

"Not so much. We like the island a lot better. There are too many cars over here. Too much noise," he answered.

We strolled along the edge of town and made it toward the back of an old building. It turned out to be the town hall of Kingfield.

A lot of the Blue Moon Dance posters were already up on the side of the building. The door was open, so we walked inside. The town hall had wood floors and a stage, kind of like a high school auditorium, but I liked the look of the building. We heard a loud truck whizz by, so we rushed across the dance floor to the window. We snuck a look outside and saw Kyle and Earl. Max was right; they drove right behind the gazebo and parked.

It was now or never.

We left the town hall and moved from tree to tree, trying to get closer to them. When someone from town walked by, we'd act normally—I'd reach out and grab his hand and we'd pretend to be on a date. We didn't want anyone to get suspicious. My blue wig was already getting us a few looks, but at least those two guys wouldn't recognize me. That's what we hoped, at least.

We made our way near the gazebo and snuck behind the dumpster. Kyle and Earl were drinking beers again. I dug out my phone and filmed what I could. We saw a bunch of barrels in the truck, covered with a dingy tarp. They were too far away to capture much audio, so I had to act fast.

I picked up a rock and pulled my arm back to throw it to the bushes, but Max grabbed my arm to stop me.

"Trust me," I whispered in his ear. He didn't stop me from throwing it on the second attempt.

The rock made enough noise for them to go take a look. I ran over and slid my phone under their truck and ran back. I made sure that it was still recording—I didn't want to miss any of what they were saying. I ran back to our hiding spot and Max looked terrified for me.

The guys returned slowly and finished their beers. I was worried they were going to take off, but they opened new beers and continued talking.

"Why did they order all these barrels if they weren't even going to use them?" Kyle asked.

Earl responded, "They were gonna, but those tree-huggers shut down the operation. They ordered the chemicals too early, I guess. Now they want no trace of this stuff around to pin it on them."

"What happens if we get caught?" Kyle asked.

"That's not an option. This thing we're doing, we'll get federal time for this. We're talking decades. Can you afford a lawyer?" Earl asked.

"Hell, no," Kyle responded.

Earl added, "We're gonna dump it at Echo Point, get the empty barrels to the landfill back here, get paid, and . . . Not. Get. Caught. Understand?"

"Yep," Kyle said. They slammed their beers and ambled toward the main street of Kingfield.

We waited for a while and then I ran to get my phone back. When I picked it up, it was still recording. I played a little back and we heard their voices pretty clearly. We had evidence. Now, we had to figure out who to give it to.

We snuck back to Max's canoe, hopped in, and got away

from shore as fast as we could. We paddled like crazy; no sleeping this time. We both worked hard until the mainland became smaller and smaller. Finally all the houses and cars looked miniature.

"I'm pretty sure we can slow down now," Max said. I felt pretty good, full of energy after what we had just done. "I'm doing fine," I said.

We paddled in silence for a while, but then a thought came to me and I shared it with Max. "What do we do with our audio? Do we play it for the police?"

"I'm not sure what would be best," he answered. "I don't know the police officers very well. A lot of them don't come to the island very often."

"Or if we can trust anyone," I added.

"I would show it to my grandfather, but I don't want to put him in harm's way," Max said.

"I could post it online and email every local and national environmental group about it," I interrupted.

"I don't understand," he said earnestly.

"I'll post the audio and send it out anonymously. Nobody will know it was us," I said proudly, then added, "I'll do it when I get home, after I create a new, anonymous account on my laptop."

"I trust you that it'll work," he finally said, but I was convinced that he didn't fully understand.

"You know, I should text or email the video to you as backup, so we have two copies of it. I have too many photos, my storage is full," I explained.

"Sure, whatever is best," he said.

"I'll need your number or email address."

"You know where I live, it's right behind the Echo Oasis bar," he said.

"No, I need your email address or phone number, not your home . . ." Then it hit me: Max didn't have a phone. He's not into technology at all.

"Are you off the grid?" I finally asked.

"I don't understand," he responded.

"Unplugged. Off the grid."

"Off the . . . I'm confused."

"Do you have a cell phone?" I finally asked.

"Oh . . . No. No, I don't. Is that okay?" he asked.

Could he and his family not afford cell phones? His grandfather's bar was always busy; they seemed like they had enough money. But Max didn't seem to own *anything* when I really thought about it. No phone. No bike. No car. I don't even think he had a wallet. All he really had was a few pairs of vintage shorts. And those weren't even his shorts, they were his grandfather's hand-me-downs.

"Yeah, it's totally okay," I finally said. "I sometimes wish none of us had these phones. They're good for emergencies, but people lived a long time without them."

"That's true," he finally added.

We paddled in silence until we made it back to the shores of Echo Island. I jumped out and dragged Max and his canoe to shore. It's surprisingly easy to do, but I still felt tough doing it. I studied how Max did it earlier and copied him.

"You're adjusting well to island life," Max told me.

"Thanks. I don't get to do this sort of thing down in the city," I said as I dropped the canoe on the beach. Not the best thing to do to a canoe. I covered my face, embarrassed.

"Don't worry, it's fine," Max said encouragingly. We tied the canoe to a post on shore and made our way down the trail.

"Why did your sister call this 'our' trail?" I asked to break the silence.

"I don't really know. I mean, we use it a lot," he answered. "It's the oldest trail on the island. My grandfather says that the animals started it. The deer, elk, and moose would come for food."

"Does Mooshy use it?"

"Probably," he answered.

"So, Mooshy is real?"

"Do you think he is?" he asked.

"Max!" I protested. He just smiled at me. "Do the animals swim from island to island?" I asked.

"Yeah, they do. In the winter they can walk on the ice. The lake freezes," he said.

"No way. This lake is way too big," I protested.

"It's true. Every year, there's an ice road that opens up once the ice is thick enough. People even drive on it," he said.

"Do *you* drive on it?" I asked.

"No. Um, I don't drive. We don't have a car," he replied.

We made it to his home and said our goodbyes. I grabbed my bike and started to walk away, but turned around to ask him another question.

"What are you doing tonight?" I asked.

"Probably helping out at the bar. What are you up to?" he asked.

I held up my phone and replied, "I'm posting this video and taking those guys down. Saving the planet."

"You are," he said and tilted his head at me. I wasn't ready for it, but he gave me one of his famous stares, looking without blinking, directly into my eyes.

"I am what?" I asked. Then he gave me a small smile, but stayed silent for a few seconds.

"You *are* saving the planet," he finally said. The staring contest started back up again, but I was too shy to keep at it. Max won the staring contest. He could beat anyone.

"I better go," I said. He didn't respond, just waved goodbye to me.

I biked toward Aunt Kat's, but remembered that my brother's laptop was closer, so I went to the supper club instead. I wanted to get that video uploaded and sent out as soon as possible.

I searched for Derek and finally found him in the kitchen. He was frying some tater tots and playing some handheld video game.

"Hey Derek, can I borrow your laptop real quick?" I asked.

"What for?" he replied.

"It's really important. I have to get an email out."

"What's wrong with your laptop?" he asked.

"I can't really tell you right now, but we need to upload this video ASAP." I held up my phone.

"Who's we? Aunt Kat said you were running around with that townie guy. Is he your new boyfriend?" he teased. Derek said "boyfriend" as if it were an evil, poisonous word.

"No, he's not my boyfriend. Okay?" He grabbed for my phone and we struggled over it.

"What's the video? You two making out?" he asked.

"Stay out of it, Derek!" I said and fought harder for my phone.

"Just let me see it!" he said.

"Let go!" I yanked the phone away, but it flew into the air. Right into the deep fryer with his tater tots.

"No!" I screamed.

"Your phone!" he exclaimed.

I clutched my head with my hands and we stared at each other for a moment. He grabbed some tongs and fished it out.

"It's cooked," he said.

"No kidding!" I yelled.

I wrapped it in a kitchen towel and shook my head. I felt like crying.

"What's the big deal? You can trade it in for a new one. Mom and Dad have insurance for you, right?" he asked.

"You're such a 'just buy another disposable one' consumer! This planet is not disposable!"

"Sorry, okay? Just calm down," he said.

"There's a really important video on there."

"Doesn't it get backed up?" he asked.

"Not if my storage is full. It's completely lost now!" I said and stormed off. A bit dramatic, I know. But I was pissed about possibly of losing all the audio evidence. I jumped on my bike and took off for Aunt Kat's house.

She was cooking dinner when I entered the kitchen.

"Hey, I haven't seen you in a while. Where've you been?" she asked. I didn't really want to explain it all to Aunt Kat.

"Derek ruined my phone, he's such an idiot!" I complained.

"You two sure like to fight," she said and dried her hands. "Can I help you with it at all?"

"Thanks, but I think it's beyond repair right now." We

didn't say too much for a minute. I think she sensed how upset I was.

"You were gone all day," she said to break the ice.

"Yeah, I was running around the island," I answered. I sat down and tried to turn my phone on. It didn't look good. Nothing happened. I thought I'd charge it and see if that would help.

"Tina said she saw you in a canoe with Thomas's grandson, Max. I didn't know you knew him," she said.

"I don't really. Not that much anyway. Do you know much about him?" I asked.

"Just from seeing him around town. And his sister Lily in the kitchen, of course. Very good kids. They don't talk much," she said.

"I know," I added.

"So, do you like him?" she asked. I knew someone was going to ask this question sooner or later. Derek sort of already did.

"I don't know," I replied. "He's so odd sometimes." I didn't feel like talking, I was so distracted by my phone. It wasn't even charging.

"Odd can be good. Just look at me," she said jokingly.

"You're a lot more fun than most," I said. Aunt Kat plunked some pasta on a plate and put it in front of me.

"Tell me if these noodles are done," she said. I tried and they tasted soft enough to me.

"I think they're perfect," I said.

"Excellent," she said as she drained them in the sink. She added some sauce and started stirring the noodles.

"You know, Max and Lily haven't had it easy. Growing up here," she said out of nowhere.

"Why's that?" I asked. I decided to leave my phone plugged in; there was nothing to do but wait. Aunt Kat was giving some background on Max and Lily, so I switched my focus.

"When Max was five, his parents were both hit by a car. They died before they ever got to the hospital."

"Oh, wow. That's so sad," was all I came up with. I couldn't imagine poor Max and Lily being so young and dealing with such a loss.

"His parents were hurt really bad, but Max's dad tried to drag his mom to safety. He took her through the woods, thinking it was the way to the hospital," she said.

"What?"

"He must have been delusional or in shock—nobody knows why he went into the woods. The driver was unconscious, so he couldn't stop him. Max's mom and dad collapsed near the beach, about a hundred feet from the water's edge."

"And then what?" I asked.

"They passed away," she whispered.

"Where were Max and Lily?" I asked.

"They were with Thomas, asleep in his house behind the bar. Their parents wanted to go for a walk at night. It was one of the last days of summer, so . . ." Aunt Kat's voice trailed off and she moved to cutting up a loaf of bread.

"I don't get it. Did they all live with Thomas behind the bar?" I asked.

"Oh no, Lily and Max's parents came from farther up north. They were visiting Thomas. Then the accident happened, so the kids wound up living with Thomas."

"Thomas seems like a very nice man," I added.

"He is. The sweetest old man this island has ever seen,"

she said. I stood and helped her bring the food to the table. "I know that there are a lot of adventures out there and before you know it, the whole day is gone, but always remember to be safe. This island can be more dangerous than the big mean city," she added.

"I know." I smiled. "Will Derek be joining us for dinner?" I asked.

"He's meeting with my accountant, so he won't be joining us. A teenager, schooling my accountant on tax law updates?" she said.

"Sounds like Derek," I groaned.

"We'll get him to join our side: the revolution to save our Mama Earth. Right?" she asked.

"Right!" I smiled at her, and she messed up my hair before we sat down to dinner.

Before bed, I tried everything I could to get my phone to work, but nothing happened. I even used a toothpick to pluck lint out of all the crevasses. We risked so much to get that audio and it was all for nothing. All the evidence lost in a stupid deep fryer.

I woke up at three in the morning in a panic. I had a dream I was swimming, but trying to get to the surface. I was running out of air and the surface looked so far away.

Max appeared in my dream and kissed me underwater to give me air. We kissed for a long time. Before I knew it, we weren't underwater anymore. I felt safe and his kissing was really fun. Like, super fun. I wished that kiss could've lasted for ten hours.

I had kissed Trevor back in the city, but I didn't like it the way I liked this.

Kissing Max in my dream felt like how I thought it was

supposed to feel. All the science stuff I said before about kissing? It still applied. But this dream? This was different.

The dream shifted gears really fast. Max was gone, and I was back underwater, swimming up and up to the surface, panicked.

I woke up, gasping for air. I put my hand on my heart and looked around the attic. I was wide awake, but terrified. I wanted to talk to Aunt Kat or even Derek, but the house was so quiet; it was almost three in the morning. I looked out the window and the moon was so big and bright, it barely looked like nighttime out there. I checked to see if my phone was properly plugged in. It was, but still no sign of life. I felt hopeless and restless.

I jumped on my bike and headed into town. Maybe Mooshy the Elk would talk to me, I don't know. I knew that I wouldn't be able to sleep for hours. The island was like a ghost town at three in the morning. It wasn't exactly a party place for young people and the bars had long been closed.

I biked up to Mooshy and locked my bike up. I talked to him, but he didn't talk back. I started to plod around town, peeking into the coffee shop and the tiny grocery store, but nobody was around anywhere. I thought for a second about Kyle and his brother and got a little nervous, but then remembered that they barely ever come onto the island.

I heard some footsteps and out of instinct, I ducked behind the coffee shop and waited. I slowly peeked around the edge of the building and realized that the footsteps belonged to Max, but he looked around like he didn't want to be seen.

He tiptoed to the window of the Tavern restaurant and crouched down to the fish in the aquarium. He looked up to a small open window above the main door and then proceeded to touch the window with both palms. He looked around again, this time with even more nervousness.

Something shifted in the air, the way it actually felt. I sensed an electricity. I could detect a strong scent of leaves and dirt. Like the way it smells when it starts to rain on a dry day.

Even though it was dark out, the moon lit up the scene and the night's color changed too; it turned sort of a yellow green. The way the sky changes before a big storm. I swore I even saw a few snowflakes again. This next part, I don't even think I believe, but I swear I saw it.

I swear it.

The water from the aquarium sort of lifted out of the aquarium and traveled up into the air, with the fish included. It traveled as if in a stream up toward the window above the door. Max was controlling it. He held his hand and concentrated on the water. All the water moved through the open window and down toward Max. It collected above his hand in a large sphere.

It was like a magician was holding a fish bowl and then snapped their fingers and *poof* all the glass was gone, but the water held its shape and the fish swam happily in circles.

I rubbed my eyes, thinking that if I closed and opened them, this surreal scene would go away and it'd just be Max standing there, answering my question with a question.

But the scene didn't change. Max moved slowly away as if he were balancing a stack of dishes on his head. Once he moved about a block away, I had no choice. I had to follow him.

Max snuck through the woods to the beach. He stood in the sand with great concentration as the sphere of water and fish made it over the lake. It hovered over the surface for a moment and the fish, one by one, jumped from the sphere and landed in the lake.

Max fell to his knees, but he kept one hand up, controlling the sphere. When the last fish jumped into the lake, the sphere grew bigger and bigger and became individual drops of water. Then it turned into a mist and dissolved into the night's air and disappeared.

The color of the sky and the electricity in the air reminded me of something. A really strong sense memory of when I had my bike accident in the rain. All those similar senses returned to me.

Max shuffled a little on his knees, and eventually collapsed on the beach. He was a couple feet from the water, so he extended his arm until he touched the small waves of the lake. I heard him exhale loudly.

Seriously, what just happened?

I know a lot of what happens on this island doesn't happen in the city. And some of it couldn't be explained. But this? This was a lot to take in. Something seemed like an answer to me, though. I felt a little relieved. I knew Max was way different than other guys my age, but now I realized why he was so different.

It was like discovering a secret about someone that only makes you like them more. A secret that they think will make you like them less, but it has the opposite effect.

Like when my friend Brooke nervously told me that she was a vegetarian. She was so used to people not understanding her that she didn't put it out there. It was a bonding moment because we were on the same side.

This was something I couldn't fully understand. But he was freeing some fish from being dinner at a restaurant, so

I bonded with that. He clearly didn't want to be seen doing it—I understood that too.

He rolled over on his back and breathed in and out; his fingers were still touching the water. I guess I didn't need an explanation. I felt a need to help him, to make him better. He clearly was not in good shape, weakened somehow by his rescue mission.

He was able to make it back to his feet. He looked behind himself, but not in my direction. I'm guessing he wanted to make sure that nobody saw this spectacular event.

Why didn't I film it on my phone? At least then, someone would believe me. I would be able to show it to Aunt Kat or Brooke. I could watch it myself to know it had really happened.

But then I remembered that my phone was a deep-fried basket of non-working technology and wouldn't take a video in the first place.

Max took a few steps and dove into the water. He didn't surface right away, so I started to worry. It seemed like minutes passed by and I got really worried.

I looked around and back at the water, but no Max. I thought that he might be hiding behind a large rock, but there were none to be seen in the strong light of the moon.

A couple minutes later, I really started to panic. I ran down to the beach and looked everywhere. Was he swimming on his back somewhere? Did I miss him coming up for air? What was happening?

I know a lot of things can be explained. I'd once read about the world record free-diving guy. He was able to hold his breath for over twenty-two minutes. Max was probably at five minutes at that point. Was he like that free diver?

Someone who practiced holding his breath? Most of those people dove in the ocean, not the lake.

Every second that ticked by, the more worried I got. I started to yell out his name. I even screamed, "Max, please!" But nothing.

I covered my face and sat down in the sand. There was nothing else to do. There must be a logical explanation of where he went, I thought. I don't care about his secret, I just wanted to see his face again. I was so worried. I didn't realize I was so attached to him already. Not knowing where he was felt like the worst feeling to me. My stomach started to hurt and my head pulsated itself into a nasty headache.

The sun was coming up soon and I didn't want to be sitting on the beach for that. I knew that if Aunt Kat found my attic room empty, she'd be worried, so I made my way back to the house. I recounted it all, trying to make sense of the whole thing.

Wednesday, July 13th

I got in so late, but I still woke up early somehow. I guess I was restless to be up. I had a lot of questions about what I had seen and I still had to get my phone to work.

Max's secret seemed like a dream to me. Did I dream the whole thing? I know that I didn't, but it seemed so unreal. Like, really unreal. How did he do all that? Was he even human?

I went down to breakfast where Aunt Kat and Derek were already fixing it.

"Need any help?" I offered.

"Perfect timing, Reesie. We just finished making it," Derek teased.

"Have a seat, we're good," Aunt Kat said.

"You can do the dishes," he said blankly.

I sat down and fidgeted with my phone. Derek placed a plate of pancakes and eggs before me.

"See how easy your job waiting tables is? I didn't even spill anything," he gloated.

"Great. You can cover my lunch shift," I countered.

"Did you get that french-fried phone to work yet?" he asked. He must have been feeling guilty; he usually never asks questions about my life.

"Thanks for your concern," I scoffed.

He grabbed the phone and charger from my hands and took off.

"Let a dude do it, okay?" he said.

What a sexist thing to say. But before I could protest, he was messing with the buttons.

"My cyber knight in shining emojis," I said and stuck my tongue out at him. He returned the favor and then focused on my phone and left the room. I think he actually did feel responsible for once. Did my annoying brother actually have a conscience?

Aunt Kat sat down and started eating with me; we ate our breakfast in silence. After she took her last bite, she put down her fork and looked at me with a serious expression. Out of nowhere, she pulled the blue wig from under the table.

"Where did you find this?" she asked. We both started laughing.

"Oh, I got that from Max," I said nervously. I didn't tell her that I had to wear it because I was hiding out from two eco-terrorist thugs. "I'm going to wear it to the dance," I added innocently.

"I like it, but will it match your dress?" she asked.

"Doesn't black go with everything?" I asked.

Aunt Kat grabbed my hand and took me away from the table. "I've got just the thing for you," she said as she led me upstairs. "I know you're sleeping in the attic, but do you remember the secret closet?" she asked.

"Secret closet?" I said to myself with confusion. She rolled her eyes at me and complained, "You forgot the secret closet? It used to be your favorite spot when you were little.

There's even a little window. Your window. You used to call it your 'me-sized window,' remember?"

"I guess I don't," I responded. She marched me into the room and past my bed. The attic was made up of white wood panels, and in a seam between the wood paneling there was a small rope. She pulled it and a section of the wall opened. It was a door, a secret one. I climbed in to find a metal rolling rack of old clothes.

"Remember the little window?" she asked.

"Sort of," I replied as I hunched over past all the old clothes.

"You take a look out the window. I'm going to find the dress that you *must* wear to the dance Friday night. Don't bump your head."

I ducked down even more and moved toward the window. I sat down and looked out at the front yard. I remembered something about that window, but I must have been five years old when I was last in that room. Around a decade ago. I used my shirt sleeve to wipe the dust off the window. I stared out, trying hard to remember. Maybe if I kept staring, the memory would come back.

"A-ha! Found it!" she said excitedly. "Come look!" I stood up and met her next to my bed. She pulled the dress from behind her back and yelled, "Ta-da!"

Ta-da was right. It was a vintage mermaid dress made out of turquoise fabric and large shiny sequins. Like, a lot of sequins. It shimmered like the sun did on the lake when it was about to set. It was more of a costume than a dress.

"Is this for Halloween?"

"Nope. The Mermaid Parade," she answered.

"The Mermaid Parade?" I asked.

"My first trip to New York . . . I wound up in the first-ever Mermaid Parade in Coney Island with my girlfriends. It was a parade where everyone dressed like mermaids."

"What?" I asked, completely confused.

"It was for some business, I don't remember," she explained as she studied the dress. "1983, I think it was. I was about your age."

Aunt Kat was full of adventurous stories like this. Just when you thought you'd heard them all, another wild story would pop back into her memory.

"I can't picture you wearing this." I shook my head.

"I sure did! I had a smaller waist back then. I bet it's your size. Will you try it on?" she begged.

"A mermaid? That is so not my style," I protested.

"Do it for me, please. It's not one of those dumb 'sexy mermaid' dresses with a bikini top. Please?" she begged. I inhaled with a little fake drama and took the dress behind the changing screen. Yes, Aunt Kat has an old-fashioned changing screen to change your clothes behind.

I looked down at the dress and laughed to myself. It looked like a dress for a musical from the 1960s, not for a science nerd and co-founder of the Earth's Last Chance Club. I started to change into the dress.

I felt like Aunt Kat was opening up to me, so I went against my shy nature and asked her a few things.

"I bet a lot of guys chased you around Coney Island while you were in this dress," I said.

"Just eight or ten hot dudes," she said jokingly.

"Not bad," I said and we laughed together.

"But now . . ." she started to add, but stopped herself.

"Now you have fifteen to twenty dudes after you?" I asked.

"Ha! No ma'am Pam. I'm taking a break from dudes for a while. It's kind of slim pickings up here."

"I guess it would be."

"No other cute redheads like Max, right?" she asked.

"Hey!" I protested

"I have to tease you, it's my duty as your aunt. But enough about guys, let's see that dress!"

As I zipped it up along the side, it seemed a little tight, but it fit snug and almost like it was made just for me. I tend to wear a lot of baggy T-shirts, so I'm not used to form-fitting clothes. Those clothes are kind of gross and I usually try to avoid them. There was a necklace made out of shells and pearls, so I put that on, too.

I put my hands over my eyes and walked out to show her. There was no mirror behind the changing screen, so I had no idea what I looked like. Aunt Kat was silent.

"Is it that bad?" I asked as I took my hands down from my face. She put her hands over her mouth, then smiled.

"Wow," was all she said at first as she exhaled deeply.

"That bad?" I asked again. She wiped her forehead and swallowed a lump in her throat.

"No. It's . . . perfect," she finally said.

"What do I do with the tail?" I finally asked.

"There's a string that holds it up when you walk around, or when you *dance*." She winked at me.

"I don't know if I should wear this to the dance."

"Of course you should," she said encouragingly.

"I better get ready for the lunch shift," I said. She perked up and laughed to herself.

"You're not wearing the mermaid dress to work, are you?" she asked.

"Uh, no," I answered.

Aunt Kat studied me in the dress a little longer.

"Tell you what . . ." she started to say. Something in her tone sounded fun.

"What?" I asked.

"You wear that dress to the dance and I'll cover your lunch shift today," she offered.

"What? Really?" I asked.

"Yeah. You know you look good in it. It's the first time you've stood up straight since you set foot on this island," she said.

"Huh?" I was confused.

"That dress gives you confidence. I want you to wear it and I want you to dance the crap out of it on Friday," she said.

I laughed at her idea, but I knew she was right. After a little more protest, I finally agreed to wear the dress to the dance. She stood up and gave me a long hug and wouldn't let go.

"Can we be done now?" I asked.

"Done? Done with what?" she asked.

"This hug. I'm not used to hugs this long," I replied.

She laughed and pinched my cheek.

"What do I wear for shoes?" I asked. She practically jumped in the air.

"Blue sequin shoes, of course!" she squealed and ran into the secret closet. One shoe after another came flying out of the closet until I finally heard, "Here they are!" She emerged with a pair of shiny blue heels and handed them over to me.

"Don't give this a second thought. You must wear these

with the dress," she demanded. I secretly thought they were amazing, but I felt like I had to protest a little more.

"But, what if—" I started to say, but she cut me off.

"I'm off to the club, gotta polish up my skills as a server!" she said as she winked at me and left the attic. "Don't wear that dress all day."

I looked down at the shimmering dress. Then I thought of Max and his secret. His five-in-the-morning magic show. How was I going to bring up the fact that I spied on him?

The lack of sleep hit me, so I changed into my pajamas and hung the dress on the door. I placed the shoes under the dress, and Aunt Kat was right: they looked awesome together. I stared at the dress and then looked to the secret closet. Aunt Kat said that the closet was my favorite place, but why couldn't I remember much about it?

I took an extra long nap, but in my dream, I never left the attic. I dreamed I was sitting on the floor of the secret room, reading a book with a flashlight. Something from the little window caught my eye. I turned off my flashlight so I would see the yard better.

I squinted my eyes and noticed someone moving toward the house. It wasn't creepy, it was the opposite. I was comforted by this figure. It was more of a memory than something new. It didn't take long for the figure to come close enough for me to focus on. It was Max.

He held his hands folded in front of him. He looked so formal, almost like he was praying. He lifted his hands up, opened them, and a small bird flew out.

The bird flew right at me and then to the roof. My eyes followed the bird, but I couldn't see it anymore. When I looked down at Max, he did nothing but put his hands in his pockets, and then gave me the smallest, sweetest smile.

His smile made me feel like nobody had ever smiled at me before. A brand new smile. Like none I had ever seen. Was I idealizing him in my dreams, or was he really that dreamy?

He kept staring directly into my eyes. With those eyes. Those intense eyes. He was definitely winning our staring contest, because I started to get uncomfortable and had to look away.

I looked up and pretended I had another shot at seeing the little bird, but of course I didn't see it. I couldn't stare into that face any longer without my cheeks turning bright red.

When I looked back down to Max, he was gone. Not walking away, but completely gone.

Vanished again.

Why was he always disappearing?

I woke up super rested physically, but still restless about Max and what he was able to do with the water the night before when he rescued those fish from becoming dinner.

Since Aunt Kat took my shift in exchange for me wearing the mermaid dress to the dance, I had the whole day free. I wanted to see if Derek had any luck with my phone, but when I checked his room, it was empty. I saw my phone, plugged in at his desk. I picked it up, but it was still completely broken.

There was just one thing to do: get some answers from Max, if I could find him.

I biked to all the major spots on the island. Asked Lily, asked Thomas. I even asked my brother. Nobody knew where Max was. I had some dinner at Kat's Club—a salad with a side of mashed potatoes, my favorite. I took off on my bike to try one more loop around the island before it got too dark.

I was about to head back when I finally spotted Max coming out of the water at Echo Point Beach. I was nervous about confronting him, but I had to get at least one answer that night.

I biked down and saw him sitting in the sand, facing out toward the sunset. He had no towel, no shirt, nothing. Only his classic uniform: his swimsuit. He had made a small campfire and he sat down on a wood log.

As I approached, he must have heard me. He turned his face to meet mine and the seriousness of his expression made me swallow a lump in my throat.

Why do we get lumps in our throats anyway? I looked it up once. Turns out it's not a lump at all. It's the body reacting to a stressful situation. Our vital organs go into a "fight or flight" moment, craving more oxygen. Our throats sort of open more near our vocal chords, allowing more air. Fight or flight? I was not going to run away. I was on a mission.

Still, I had to face those eyes. They seemed to look right into my brain. Right into my heart. I think he sensed, on some level, what was coming. What I needed to know. We both played it cool for a little bit, though. You can't just come out and ask, "Are you a wizard? Are you part fish? Are you, like, Aquaman's nephew?"

"How was your swim?" I asked as I sat down. Boring icebreaker, I know. But I had to start somewhere.

"I loved it," he answered. I could tell he meant it. Nobody in the city really said what they felt, and most don't say they love things very often. Unless it's about ice cream or a pair of jeans or a famous actor. They don't often say how they really feel.

Max really did love it. There was nothing ironic or sarcastic about him. It was like he never learned how to be. He meant everything he said.

"That's good to hear," was all I could come up with. We were silent for a few moments.

"I know you saw me last night," he came out and said. I took a deep breath, shocked. Well, that was easy. We were definitely going to talk about it, like, right now.

"How did you know?" I asked.

"I heard you calling my name while I swam underwater," he replied.

"You heard me?"

"Yeah" he said.

"Can you tell me how you do all that? How you controlled the water?" I asked.

"I'm not allowed to tell you, but if you ask me questions, I'm also not allowed to lie." He looked down to the sandy beach and continued, "What would you like to know?"

"Did you control the water last night? With the fish in it?" I asked, not knowing where to start.

"I know I can trust you, Theresa. Not to tell anyone. Please."

"You can trust me."

Max took a deep breath. He played with the sand on the beach, but eventually smoothed it all out.

"Yeah. I did. I controlled the water," he responded.

"Well, how?"

"It's just something I can do. I was born being able to do it in small ways, then it got stronger."

"What else can you do?"

"I can't tell you," he said. This should've made me frustrated, but I had to act like a lawyer and ask the right questions.

"My first day up here, that was you waterskiing, wasn't it?"

"That was me, but I didn't use skis. There wasn't a boat. I was just gliding on the surface of the water for a few seconds, having fun. I didn't think anybody would see me."

"Can you breathe under water?" I tried.

"Yes."

"For how long."

"As long as I can breathe out of water."

"Are you, like, a mermaid or merman or a siren or something?" He smiled at that question. We were starting to feel relieved to have some truths come out.

"I don't have scales or anything."

"Does your body change? Do you get, like, a fishtail?"

"No, my body stays the same." I had a million questions to ask, but I didn't know which ones to ask first.

"Are you a Native American?" I tried, but thought that might be a dumb question. He didn't think it was dumb, he answered sincerely.

"My ancestors have been here a long, long time, but I'd say I'm not Native American in the ways that you've learned."

"What do you call yourself?"

"Max," he answered seriously. I laughed, but he just smiled at me.

"My real name is Alvo, but I go by Max. It's just easier. Thomas didn't want people asking a lot of questions about such a unique name. Lily picked it out for me when we first came to the island."

Was this all really happening? In an attempt to make it more real, I kept going.

"Do you want me to call you Alvo?"

"Would you like to?" he asked.

"It sort of fits you, but I'm so used to Max."

"Max works for me," he said.

"Does Lily have another name?"

"Her real name is Lilja, but Lily was better for everyone here," he answered.

"That day I had my bike accident. Did you prevent me from getting injured?"

"I did."

"How?" I asked. Max reached over and held my hand.

"I used the rain drops to catch you, slow you down, and cushion your fall," he responded.

"How come I don't remember much of it?"

"Maybe it happened too fast?"

"I don't believe you," I protested. "Did you do a mind eraser type of thing on me?"

"No," he said. After a long pause, he kept going, "Not exactly."

"Huh?"

"I rearranged some of the water in your brain, so you wouldn't remember a second or two. We can do that for really short memories."

"You can take a blip out?" I asked.

"What's a blip?"

"A little chunk of time," I answered.

"Yeah. I guess we can remove a blip."

"Whoa. That's so . . . wow!" I said.

"Can Lily and Thomas do what you do?"

"Lily can, but Thomas can't," he responded. I wrinkled my brow.

"Why can't Thomas?" I asked.

"He's not like us. He's like you," he answered.

I started to put it all together and then asked, "He's not

your real grandfather, is he?"

"No. He's not. He is now. But we're not related by blood," he answered. "He's been taking care of us for a long time. He knew my parents really well."

I didn't want to talk about his parents dying, because I didn't want to make him sad. But he brought it up instead.

"Thomas started taking care of Lily and me after my parents died. They were hit by a car," he said.

"I heard about that from my aunt," I finally said.

"Lily and I were asleep when it happened. My parents tried to get to the water's edge, but they were too injured," he explained.

"Why didn't they go to the hospital?" I asked.

"We can't do stuff like that. They would've studied them. They would've locked them away in a lab somewhere. The water heals us. It would've healed their injuries. Only, they didn't make it in time."

"Is that why you touched the water last night?" I asked.

"Yeah. When I manipulate the water, it weakens me and I have to get that energy back from the lake. Does that make sense?" he asked.

"Yeah. Oddly, it does," I said and continued, "I'm so sorry you lost your parents."

"Thank you. I know you are," he said.

I drew a circle in the beach sand and asked more questions.

"Where is the rest of your family?"

"They're all over, mostly under the water, a lot of my close relatives are near an underwater cave north of Outer Island. Have you heard of that?" he asked.

"I've seen it from the ferry. The tour guide pointed it out.

It's pretty far away, right?" I asked.

"Yeah, about ten miles," he answered.

I somehow found the strength to go against my own shyness and keep questioning him.

"Why did your family come to Echo Island?" I asked.

"The waters here have stronger powers for us than what circles the other islands. But something was poisoning the lake. My parents were sent to the island to find out more about the poison. And to stop it."

"Poison?"

"Yes, over ten years ago. A factory on the mainland was dumping their waste in the water. And now—"

"It's happening again," I finished his sentence.

"Yes, it's happening again," he repeated.

We both stopped talking and looked up to the sky. It was starting to get dark and the stars were already out. I felt pretty helpless and I sensed that Max did too. Big forces were out to damage the pristine lake, and who were we? Just a couple teenagers. One with a big secret and one with a mangled cell phone that held the evidence to stop the damage. What were we going to do? What we were trying to do could put us in danger, but if we did nothing, many other people and animals and fish would surely suffer or die. Suffer and die for years and years.

Max held up his hand and summoned a very small isolated rain shower, just enough to magically extinguish our little campfire.

"We should get you home," Max finally said.

We stood up and headed down a trail. We walked in silence for a bit. I wanted an easy solution to all this. I wanted to resolve everything faster. I wanted results. I was so used to getting things so fast. A text message, an email, a package overnight or in one hour. We were able to do anything, right?

"Why couldn't we use your powers to stop them? Erase those polluters' brains? Get more help from your family? Couldn't we easily take them all down?" I asked.

"It doesn't work like that. Somebody always has to pay for it and it's usually my people," he countered. "We'd all become weak, then we'd be captured and they'd expose us and destroy *all* of us."

I hadn't seen this side of Max. I always knew he had strong opinions, but he seemed angry for the first time.

"I know, but—" I started and he cut me off.

"What about you? What about your people? You're supposed to be so smart and evolved and civilized? What civilized people would ruin their own home, poison the very water that gives them life? You have all the information in those screens you stare into, but you do nothing about it!"

"Max, wait—" I tried to reason with him.

"You're supposed to get smarter with the more information you have, but it's the reverse with your kind! You know more and more, but care less and less. You don't care what happens to all those plastic or poisonous things you toss out of your cars, do you?" Max stormed off past me down the trail.

"Wait, come back!" I yelled and ran after him. He stopped and turned to me and started talking again.

"My real grandfather, Tibor, he sent my parents here to stop what the humans were doing and look what happened. My parents are gone. Tibor wanted to start a war with your people, but my parents convinced him not to. They said that there was another way. They were wrong," he said.

"Max, I'm on your side. Let's figure out a plan. The dance

is in two days; we have time to stop the polluters. We need a plan. Let's calm down and . . ." He stormed off again, but I caught up.

"My grandfather is getting impatient. If those guys dump that toxic stuff, there's no telling what he'll do," he said.

"What do you mean?" I asked.

"You will not be spared. He'll take out any human in his way, every human on this island."

I grabbed Max by the face and focused on his eyes. "We're going to stop them. We're going to take care of it. We can do it if we work together. We have two days to come up with a plan," I said.

Our foreheads were almost pressed together and we were both breathing heavily. I felt all his anger and frustration and hopelessness. The stakes were raised, but I was ready to fight and Max had been ready for a long time. Our breathing slowed down and I put my hand on his heart in an attempt to slow it down.

The next logical step? I had to kiss him. If we were going to stop the lake from being poisoned and save all the inhabitants of the island, those were pretty big things, right? A good make-out session seemed like a minor thing. So I went for it. We kissed and kissed and kissed.

When Trevor used to kiss me, he was too slobbery, way too messy. It was like kissing a golden retriever.

Max was way different. I could've kissed him for at least thirty-six hours straight. Maybe longer.

The world record kiss lasted fifty-eight hours, thirty-five minutes and fifty-eight seconds. It happened in Thailand on Valentine's Day in 2013. Maybe the record is broken by now, but I think Max and I could have lasted longer than fifty-eight hours.

Was Max controlling the water in my brain and heart and body so I'd feel this way? The average human is about 60 percent water, so it would be easy for him to do. But if he was controlling the water in my body, it would've weakened him.

That was not the case. His kissing got more and more passionate the longer we kissed. As you know, I used to think kissing and the passing along of testosterone from the male to female was so gross and all that stuff. But this wasn't just your ordinary kiss.

Raindrops started to fall all around us, but I felt none. I stopped kissing him to look around and noticed that the ground directly around us was dry. I looked up and there appeared to be an invisible dome around us, protecting us from rain.

I looked to Max, the cause of our magical umbrella against the rain, and he smiled.

We stopped to look up at the ceiling of our clear bubble that was made of rain. I reached up and touched the roof of the magical dome with my index finger. A little drop of rain moved down to my palm; I brought it down for both of us to examine. We looked at it and smiled and then I watched as Max levitated the drop of water back up to the dome of water, where it joined all the other rain. I looked him in the eye.

"What do we do now?" I asked.

"Can we just stay a little longer?"

"And do what?"

"Be with each other?" he asked.

"Okay," I said.

I took his hand and held it; we both stared down at our hands and were quiet. The noise of the rain faded away and we looked around and felt the silence. The rain smelled so clean and natural.

"I'm sorry I got so upset a minute ago," he broke the silence.

"It's understandable," I said.

"It's just that I get so—" he started to say, but I interrupted him.

"You don't have to explain," I said, and we started to hike down the trail together.

"It's . . . I know who you are, I've always known what kind of person you are and . . ." he said.

"It's okay. We're on the same team. I'm not like most humans," I said.

"I know," he said and stopped me. I squeezed his hand. "Let's go," I said, and we went down the trail together.

Max accompanied me all the way to Aunt Kat's house. When we arrived, we looked up to the moon.

"Look, it's almost the full moon," he pointed out. "Thomas and Lily are waiting for me. I don't want them to worry," he said.

"I understand," I said. We kissed again and said our goodbyes.

Once inside, I zipped past Aunt Kat and Derek because I wanted to write down all the details of the kiss before I forgot them. There was so much to remember. I plopped down in the secret room by the window. I also wanted to get one last look at Max as he left the yard. I tapped on the window and he turned to wave at me.

Max in the front yard.

Just like the dream I had earlier. Me looking out the little window at Max looking up at me. No bird this time. Just a cute boy, waving to me. It was something more than a dream, something so familiar.

Was it déjà vu? Science rejects déjà vu as the brain just misfiring, an anomaly of memory. Whatever it was, I couldn't figure it out. I touched the window with my palm and waved goodbye to Max.

I hopped into bed and couldn't stop thinking of Max and all his super-sized secrets. A million other questions popped into my head. Questions I should have asked him: Do you miss your parents? Can you stay out of water as long as you want? Do you live as long as humans? Longer? Shorter? Do you have a Social Security number? Seriously, though, what was really going on?

I went back to the thinking about his kiss, because that was more fun. I thought, *This is what all those corny books and movies were trying to tell me!* I never believed them, because it had never happened to me.

Even better than kissing, I had found another ally. All those days of Brooke and me getting yelled at for our environmental ideals, I thought we'd be fighting the fight forever. That nobody else would get where we were coming from.

Now, I met someone who not only got it, but he challenged other thoughts that I had, pushed me into looking at the planet in another way. I met someone who would fight *with* me. And someone who'd *kiss* me as we were fighting!

I couldn't help it: I started kissing my pillow, pretending it was Max. I was really going for it when I heard Derek's voice.

"Wow, you *really* like that pillow. Gross!" he screamed.

I jumped up and saw my brother standing in the doorway.

I immediately threw a bunch of pillows at him and screamed back.

"Get out! Get out of here! What are you doing here?"

"Aunt Kat sent me up here. We're watching a movie and she wanted me to invite you down, but I'll tell her you're busy 'getting busy' with a pillow," he said.

"I'm going to kill you!" I screamed again. We both burst out laughing; there was nothing else we could do.

"Get out. I'm going to bed," I said.

"Yeah, right. You're going to get it on with that poor innocent pillow!" he teased.

"Out!" I yelled and closed the door.

I turned and laughed to myself. What could be more embarrassing than your brother seeing you kiss a pillow? I picked up the pillows and looked around at my special little attic room. A thunderstorm had started. The rain was hitting the roof of the house pretty hard. The lightning lit up the room.

I climbed into the secret room and sat next to my little window. I felt so safe and comforted even though there was a massive storm outside. I worried about Max getting home on foot, but then I remembered he was probably meandering home in a dry bubble, protected from all the rain. I smiled to myself at the idea of that.

Then I thought to myself, *Could all this stuff really be happening to me?* Yes, it was, it wasn't something I read in a book. I was living all of it.

Thursday, July 14th

I woke up in my little secret room. I guess at some point in the night, I had bundled up some clothes and used them as a pillow and fell asleep. I thought about Max; I was really knocked over the head by what had happened the day before. But that was all in the past now. Today was all about getting back to reality.

The alarm on my phone went off, so I smacked it out of instinct, but it kept beeping. I swiped the alarm away. I couldn't believe that the alarm was working. If that worked, maybe the audio file would too.

I pressed a bunch of buttons, but only the alarm would work. I ran down the stairs with excitement.

"My phone is coming back to life!" I screamed, but in my excitement, I dropped the phone and it bounced down the stairs. Derek picked it up and shook it next to his ear, like it had pennies in it or something.

I tried to grab it away from him, but he held it up high. He put his hand over it and pretended to do a magic spell on my phone.

"Dear Theresa's phone, you better work or we'll drive you to the mall and demand a newer better version of you. Pow!"

He handed the phone back to me, but when I looked down at it, it was completely blank.

"Your magic spell didn't work," I said and restarted it.

"Be patient," he said. We both stared into it and then we heard it: it made its original chiming noise. My heart started pounding really fast. The screen lit up! Did the bouncing down the stairs jump-start it? Either way, there was no denying it:

My phone was working again!

I locked myself in the bathroom, away from Derek, and I was able to find the audio and hit play. I barely believed it: the audio recording started playing!

"It works!" I screamed and turned it off right away. I didn't want Derek to know about the audio. I swung open the bathroom door and waltzed past him.

"I told you I'd fix it," he bragged.

"I'm pretty sure it wasn't your magic trick."

"What's that recording you played?"

"None of your business!" I yelled back to him as I ran out the door.

I had it. I had the proof of Earl and Kyle's plan to dump the toxic chemicals in the lake. Who should I show it to? Do I call the EPA? What to do now?

I hopped on my bike and set out to get some advice from Aunt Kat. As I rode, I passed the spot where I met George, the environmental contract guy. Maybe he would get my audio to the right people instead of posting it anonymously online?

I had to get it to someone fast; they were planning the chemical dump for the following night! Plus, who knows how much longer my fried phone would even work.

I talked to Aunt Kat in her office about George. She said he was part of the fight against fracking, but he didn't officially take a side because he had to stay objective for his research.

"But he's on our side," she confided in me.

"Do you know where he's staying? I have an audio file to play for him," I said.

"What file?" she asked.

I played the audio for her and she was understandably shocked.

"Why didn't you tell me about this?" she asked.

I didn't want to tell her about my life getting threatened and that I wanted to resolve it all myself in order to keep her out of harm's way. I was almost sixteen; I wanted to figure it out myself.

"I don't know. I should've, I guess," was all I said.

"Don't worry about it now. Show it to George. He's staying at the Cedar Bark Lodge. I'd show it to him as soon as you can. Just don't do anything to put yourself in danger. Wait, I'll come with you," she offered.

"I can do it. You're busy here," I said. She gave me a look of worry.

"I'll be fine," I was out the door before she could protest.

I zipped over to the lodge and found George working on his computer in the lobby. I reintroduced myself and he remembered me. I was pretty nervous as I played him the audio file. He was very alarmed by it. His face flushed and I asked him, "Should we upload it to your computer?" He studied my phone.

"It looks like your phone is too damaged for that," he said. "But we need to get this phone to the Department of

Natural Resources, as soon as possible. They'll know what to do."

"Where are they?" I asked.

"There's a field station on the mainland, not far from the ferry dock. I'm going across the lake in an hour; we could deliver your phone together. I'm sure they have a rap sheet a mile long on those guys."

"Did those guys work for you last week?" I asked.

"They were supposed to, but I fired them. They didn't seem trustworthy in the end," he answered.

"What were they going to do for you?" I asked.

"Help me take water samples from around the island," he answered.

"Do you know someone at the Natural Resources office?" I asked.

"Not personally, but I've been there before," he said.

"I'm a little worried about going into Kingfield. Those guys might see me."

"Did they threaten you?" he asked.

"No, but I think they know that I heard something," I said.

"Oh, that's not good."

"Would you take it there for me?" I asked.

"If you're okay with me bringing it alone." I handed him my phone.

"Of course," I said.

"Their conversation says it all. I can testify that it's their voices. It'll be enough to land them in jail before they do any harm," he said.

I exhaled with relief. I was so excited to have helped prevent this, I couldn't stop smiling. I was almost on the verge of tears; I covered my face and shook it off. George squeezed my shoulder with support.

"You did a good thing, Theresa," he said.

"I wanted to do what's best for the island and the lake."

"I'll let you know as soon as they're taken into custody. Okay?" he said.

"Okay. Thank you, um, for helping," I said.

"Of course," he replied and smiled at me. "Sure you don't want to come with? The next ferry will be here soon. You deserve the credit for this," he said.

"No, that's okay. I don't want the attention," I said. And that was true. I wasn't doing this to be the hero of the island, I was happy to just be part of it. George made my introvert nature come out; he could have the five minutes of glory.

I said my goodbyes to George and left the hotel feeling like a ginormous weight had been lifted off me. I had been experiencing so much altschmerz lately.

Altschmerz is a feeling of weariness with the same old issues. What I wanted was more liberosis, a desire to care less about things. I wanted to tell Max the good news, tell Brooke, tell everyone!

I felt like celebrating. I was on a beautiful island and it was time to have fun for a while. Be a tourist. George was going to get my evidence to the right people, to stop a huge environmental catastrophe.

First things first, though: I had to share my news with Max. If it wasn't for him, I would have never been able to get the proof to stop those polluters. Plus, I wanted to see that sweet face and have fun without trying to save the lake or the island or the planet.

I found Max at his grandfather's bar. He was washing

dishes with a white apron on. It's the closest thing to a shirt I'd seen him wear.

He didn't see me at first, so I sort of studied him. I'm embarrassed to say this, but seeing him with a little more clothes on made him look even cuter. That's if you can call an apron a piece of clothing.

At that second, he turned to face me. He dried his hands on his apron and smiled at me.

He said nothing, but strode straight toward me. I fidgeted a little, secretly planning an escape from his direct approach, but I gave in. He hugged me and kissed me on the neck, and whispered in my ear.

"You must have good news."

"I do," I said.

I told him all about my phone miraculously coming back to life and me handing it off to George to get those losers busted. He was as excited as I was and we kissed. We did a little laughing, but we mostly kissed.

I swear it was unintentional, but I ripped his apron while we were kissing. We stopped to look at the apron, and his grandfather, Thomas, turned the corner and found us.

"Uh-oh. Sorry. Pretend I didn't interrupt you," he said and returned back to the bar.

"Let's go," Max said.

"What about the dishes?" I asked.

"All done!"

We ran into the sunny bar. Thomas was stocking beer and the sun was shining through the windows. A group of fishermen came in and ordered beers. Max gave Thomas a hug and I kissed him on the cheek and we started to head out.

"Where are you all off to?" Thomas asked.

"Gone swimming!" Max yelled back.

"Its like 'gone fishing' but more fun," I added. And we were off.

We rode bikes into the center of town and made a pit-stop at Mooshy. Max climbed up him again and pretended that Mooshy was a horse.

"I wish I had my phone, I'd take your picture. What you're doing is not normal behavior," I said.

"What is normal behavior?" he asked.

"I haven't figured that out yet," I teased as I accidentally stepped in a little rain puddle.

Max noticed and smiled down at me. I looked up confused. What was he thinking now? He looked around secretly for bystanders, but there was nobody around. The ferry was a few minutes away.

Max used his powers to levitate the puddle up toward him—with me attached! It was like I was rigged to some special effects ropes. I was levitated along with the puddle right up to his eye level. I closed my eyes and he kissed me with the smallest kiss imaginable. A magical peck that was extra special because it turned the whole kiss into a slow motion movie-style kind of thing.

"Will you join me, Theresa?" he whispered.

"Yes," I responded as I climbed onto Mooshy behind Max. I put my arms around his waist and rested my head on his back. I closed my eyes and listened to his heart beating slowly. I noticed it speed up a little bit.

"When are you leaving for home?" he asked.

"On Sunday," I replied. I could feel his stomach muscles tighten when I said that. Talk about a mood shift for the both of us.

"Three days away, Sunday?" he asked and I swallowed a lump in my throat. I understood the science behind why we all get lumps in our throat. I told you about it before. This didn't seem like science at all. It felt like 100 percent emotions. I wasn't used to this.

"Yeah, this Sunday," I answered.

Neither one of us said anything after that. I didn't know what he was thinking, but I knew what I was feeling and it wasn't good. It was like someone was balancing a ton of bricks on my chest.

The ferry landed at the dock and a whole new group of tourists jumped off. Families, young couples, old couples. They were all heading for us. I was thankful that they were there; we needed something to snap us out of what we were feeling. At least I needed something. I could tell Max was feeling something, too.

"Ready to go swimming?" I finally asked.

Max turned to face me and his eyes were so wounded that it almost took my breath away. There was so much sadness, his eyes looked extra large and intense. It was too much for me to handle, so I looked down at my hands.

"I'm not ready for you to go back to the city," he said. He grabbed my hand and held it. It was so warm and comforting. I still didn't look him in the eye. I focused on his hand instead. A tear started to form in my eye and I wiped it away as fast as I could.

"Can we go to Echo Point and just, I don't know, swim and have fun?" I asked.

"That's up to you," he answered. He was no longer answering my questions with questions. Maybe he thought that we didn't have time to waste. We needed to answer the questions right away, so we would have more time together.

"Yeah, that's where I want to go," I said. He jumped down from the Mooshy statue and helped me down.

For some reason, Max insisted that I ride on his handlebars, facing him. I was a little scared, but it gave me a chance to be face to face with him a little more. He biked and I enjoyed the ride. I loved facing him, watching him pedal and look so concentrated on the road.

My parents would have died if they had seen me like that. It was way too dangerous, but I felt safe with Max. Not just because of his special powers, but because of his seriousness. He was determined to get us to the water safely. I knew in the back of my mind that we'd be fine, no matter what happened.

An older couple in a vintage convertible passed us and the lady waved to me right as they went by. I waved back, which meant I was only holding on with one hand. The wind was blowing my hair all over the place. It was so reckless and so awesome, I have to admit.

"Almost there," Max finally said. I slowly moved my forehead to his and our foreheads gently touched.

"Don't crash the bike! Promise?" I screamed.

"I promise!" Max yelled back. We sped down a windy hill and I screamed most of the way down.

"Whoooaaaa!"

"Do you trust me?" Max hollered.

"Yes!"

"Face the front!" he demanded.

"No!"

"Trust me. Nothing will happen."

"How?" I asked.

"Spin around," he said and I gave him a "no way is this going to work" look.

"You're going to be fine. I have a surprise for you," he said.

I slowly started to spin forward on the handlebars, but it took a while. I was a nervous wreck, but I somehow made it around to face forward, screaming, "No!" or "Whoa!" or "Help!" as I did.

We got closer and closer to a long wooden dock, but Max wasn't slowing down.

"When we start down the dock, I want you to stand. And when we reach the end, I'm going to slam on the brakes and you're going to dive into the water, okay?" he hollered up to me.

"No. Way. Not a chance!" I yelled back at him.

"Do you trust me?" he asked.

"Of course!" I said as we started down the dock on the bike at top speed.

"Okay, stand!" he screamed.

I don't know what got into me, but I did it. It was exciting enough for me to ride on the handlebars, because trust me—that was plenty for a city girl who always aced her science tests.

I threw all the rules of physics into the trash as I crouched on the handlebars holding tight with my hands. I slowly started to stand up. I felt Max's hand on my back, anchoring me. I finally let go of the handlebars and eventually made it completely upright.

I was standing straight up on a moving bike's handlebars!

I screamed like a wild crazy person because that's exactly how I felt. Like a crazy person, what was I doing?

"Ready to dive?" Max asked.

I looked straight ahead and put my arms up into the air. I focused hard on the water. "I'm ready."

Max slammed on the brakes and I went flying into the water like a professional diver. The entry into the water was so smooth, it felt so great and so perfect and so . . . flat-out fun. Pretty much the most fun I've ever had. I was now a daredevil! If only Brooke or my brother or my parents had seen this. Wait, maybe not my parents. But I wish I had more witnesses, because I felt 100 percent *bad ass*!

I swam along underwater and when I slowed down, I opened my eyes and came face to face with Max. I'm guessing he used his powers to speed past me underwater.

We slowly came together to embrace and kiss. He must've sensed that I was running out of oxygen, because he swam us up to the surface where I inhaled with relief and laughter. I breathed and laughed and breathed and laughed.

I was so relieved and full of adrenaline at the same time. I just shook my head and screamed at Max, "I can't believe I did that! I can't believe it!"

"But you *did* do it!"

"I was flying!"

"You were." he said. We both laughed out of relief and excitement. I had too much energy to stay still, so I splashed him in the face and swam off to the dock, laughing. He followed me and we both held on to the dock. We caught our breath and slowed down our heart rates.

We looked out on the lake and I thought about what I had just done. I thought about myself when I was younger. I was super adventurous and fearless and wild. The older I got, the more careful I became. But my younger self always kept up with my older brother on all those outdoorsy things, even out-running him most of the time. My wild ride on Max's handlebars wasn't really that surprising to me, when I really thought about it. That sense of adventure was always inside me. I guess I sort of forgot I had it.

"I wish you didn't have to go," he said quietly.

"I do, too. I really do," I said. We didn't say anything else for a while; I think we were trying to slow down the time we had left with each other. Max and I spent the rest of the day doing every single tourist thing related to water.

We swam with inner tubes.

Swung on a rope swing.

Jumped off a cliff.

Dove off the dock.

Did handstands underwater.

Kissed behind a waterfall.

Made a fire on the beach.

And dried off in the sun at the end of the dock.

At one point I fell asleep briefly on the dock and woke up to a mini picnic.

"What's all this?" I asked with disbelief.

"I stopped to get us some food," he replied.

"How long was I asleep?"

"About twenty minutes," he replied.

"But how did you . . ." I stopped myself because I now knew how he got around so fast. He could be like a human torpedo underwater. It probably only took him two minutes to get there and back. Such a weirdo, that Max. But how awesome? I was getting used to how special he was, but it still felt like a fantasy.

We ate the snacks and hung out in the sun until we were warm and swimsuits were dry again. The sun was setting and there was so much I still didn't know about Max. I went back into investigative reporter mode.

"Are you really sixteen?" I blurted out.

"Yeah."

"Why are you so polite and old-fashioned? Are you sure you're not, like, eternal or something?"

"Nope, I was born sixteen years ago," he responded.

"Good, because if you were ninety years old, that'd be creepy." We both laughed together.

"Definitely still sixteen," he said.

"So, do you, uh, do this for all the girls you meet?"

"Huh?" he asked.

"Do you make all the girls stand on top of your handlebars?"

"You're the first."

"Have you ever had a girlfriend?"

"I haven't. I usually don't interact with people very much."

"No cute girls on the island?"

"I haven't made very many friends on the island," he replied.

"Do you miss your people and your grandfather?"

"I do. But . . ."

"But what?" I said. Max looked out on the water.

"He's so angry now. After my parents died, he changed. My mom and dad were so close to the water that night of the accident. So close."

"What would have happened?" I asked.

"My grandfather, Tibor, would have felt their presence had they touched the water. They would have been saved. Now, he wants someone to blame."

I reached out and touched his hand and said, "I understand." Then a thought popped into my head. That thought was the bitter cold of winter. This far north, it got to below zero often.

"What do you all do in winter? I still don't believe that this lake can freeze over," I said.

"It just does. It gets really cold."

"Then what do you do?" I said, worried.

"We stay very deep underwater."

"Don't you get cold?"

"We don't. Our bodies adjust. And we can warm the water if we want to. We sometimes sleep in the underwater caves to dry off, but we don't have to," he replied.

"Where do you normally sleep? In the water? In a bed?"

"If we're not in the caves, we're sleeping very deep in the water. It's very dark and quiet down there, very relaxing. I can sleep in a bed, but I'm more comfortable at the bottom of the lake," he said with a small smile.

I was dumbstruck. How was all this be possible? The more questions I had, the stranger he and his people seemed. It was so odd, but at the same time, I didn't care. I knew that I cared for him and he cared for me and we both felt things very deeply.

He was a unique person and he made me feel the same way. With him, I didn't disappear into a crowd on the sidewalk. I felt like he really saw the true me when he looked me in the eye. He even seemed to see a better version of me. Someone that I could strive to be.

We sat silently for a while and watched the water, the small waves, and the sun. I thought about the Blue Moon

Dance. It was something I dreaded, but Aunt Kat expected me to be there, dressed as a mermaid.

I looked at Max and thought of something. What if I wanted to be old-fashioned like him? Maybe I wanted a traditional event for us to share together. After so many years of excluding myself from stuff like the dance, deep down, I sort of wanted to belong to the bigger group and fit in.

And basically just have fun. We didn't have much time left together and we didn't have to worry about those thugs anymore. Before I could stop it, the words blurted out of my mouth.

"Will you be my date to the dance?"

"The dance on the mainland?" he asked.

"Yeah."

"Sure, I'd love to be your date."

"You will?" I said with excitement.

"Of course." He smiled. "But . . ."

"But what?"

"I've never been to a dance. What do I wear?" he asked innocently.

"Do you have any dress clothes or a suit?"

"No, I don't."

"I bet Thomas has something you can wear. Either way, we'll figure something out. Okay?" I said.

"What are they like?" he asked.

"Dances can be pretty corny, but we're going to make it fun. Okay?"

"Okay." He looked down at my hand and squeezed it.

"Have you been to one?" he asked.

"I have, but I never danced."

"What did you do?"

"I just stood on the side and watched."

"Watched everyone dance?" he asked.

"Yeah."

"You will dance this time," he demanded.

"Okay, maybe," I said and laughed at his bossiness. I could tell he wasn't trying to be bossy. He was being Max, sweet and protective; he wanted me to have a good time.

We walked the bike back to Aunt Kat's house. He asked about my life in the city and I asked more about his life in the water. His community was like any other community, but with underwater caves and no need to breathe oxygen.

I invited him to dinner, but when we arrived at the house, Aunt Kat and Derek were gone. Just a note, saying that they were at the supper club. She had packed up some leftovers for me in the fridge and there was plenty for Max and me. We heated up the food and I had an idea.

"Want to see my secret room?" I asked.

"Secret room?" he asked.

"Follow me." We took our food and climbed into my secret attic room and sat on the floor to eat. We were pretty hungry after the long day and we ate almost in silence.

Usually, I would get uncomfortable eating without talking a little, but I didn't get that way with Max. I finished everything on my plate right before Max did. He grabbed my plate from me and set it next to him. He looked around the room and focused on the little window.

"I remember this window," he said.

"You do? What do you mean? From the other night?" I asked.

"When you were younger, I brought you something. Do you remember?" he asked.

"When I was younger? I, uh . . . I don't get it."

"I brought you that bird. The one that hit the window at the supper club," he said.

Just then, I remembered it.

All of it.

It was one of my earliest, saddest memories. It was locked away in my brain, but now it was completely free.

I was five years old and my mom and I were eating at Kat's Club. A bird hit the window on the back patio. It was too injured to live much longer, so my mom took it away in a napkin and told me to stay put. I had never seen her face look so serious.

My brother and dad were out fishing, so there was nobody there to stop me from following my mom. I found her near some bushes. She was crying. She looked over and saw me. The look on her face was so somber and her eyes were so focused that it terrified me. Neither one of us could hold that intensity, so she looked down at her feet; my eyes followed hers. She had wrapped the bird in the napkin and had stepped on it.

I went mad with anger and sadness and confusion. I didn't comprehend at that age that she was showing great compassion by putting the bird out of its misery. I just knew I needed to run away. I ran into the woods, crying. My mother chased after me, caught me, and tried to explain, but I was inconsolable.

She had somehow managed to get me back to Aunt Kat's house and up into my attic bed. I wasn't able sleep, so I crawled into the secret room with the tiny window and stared out into the night. That's when it all came together:

Max.

The bird.

The front yard.

The tiny window.

"The bird that hit the window at the restaurant?" I asked Max, with tears welling in my eyes. "When I was five?"

"Yeah. That bird," he answered.

"I dreamed about that night," I told Max. "I thought that was a dream. Did that really happen? Did you bring me another bird?"

"I brought you the bird that hit the window," Max answered.

The thought was too much for me to comprehend, yet I knew it was 100 percent true. Max was too honest to make anything up. Too sincere about something so serious.

"That bird died, didn't it? How did you bring it back to life? My mom crushed it," I asked. It was so hard to believe.

"I healed it in the lake. I was wandering in the woods by the supper club when I saw how upset you were and I wanted to help."

I covered my face and wiped away some tears.

"Do you remember me standing right there?" Max pointed out the window.

"Yeah, I do," I said.

"I wanted to show you that the bird was okay. Alive."

I covered my mouth with a feeling of shock and happiness.

"It flew right at me. I can't believe that. I can't . . ." I didn't finish my sentence and shook my head in disbelief.

We sat in silence for a few moments. Max looked out the window; He didn't like all the attention. He looked over at me again and smiled.

Those eyes.

That smile.

He was too much for me.

"I didn't see you again until this year," he finally said. "Why didn't you come back to the island earlier?"

"I don't know, really. I think my parents kept putting it off for another year and then another. Derek and I begged them to come back, but we gave up after a while. Ten years later, here we are."

"Yeah," Max said and looked out the window. "I kept hoping that I'd get to see you again. I almost gave up on the idea and then there you were, piling trash on the Mooshy statue."

I laughed. "That must've been a nice picture."

"It was," he said.

It suddenly registered that he said he "almost gave up on seeing me again." After ten years? He was still hoping to see me after ten years? Ever since we were five? I did the math in my head again, but I still couldn't believe it. My face must've flushed, or maybe I looked sick to my stomach.

"Are you okay?" Max asked.

"Yeah, uh, getting a little tired," I answered. "I'll be right back. Uh, stay here. Okay?"

I darted out of the tiny secret room and ran to my bed. I grabbed all the pillows and held them tight against my chest. I tried to slow down my breathing. I looked back to make sure Max wasn't watching. I just needed to calm myself down, make sense of my emotions. I wasn't used to this kind of thing. I never imagined anyone waiting for me for that long.

I put most of my faith in science and not affairs of the heart. But it was safe to say that Max was changing that for me. How could he not? He was proving all these "romantic" notions to be true. If my time with Max was put against the scientific method, it would surely pass. Once all the facts were on the table, even Einstein would approve.

I took a deep breath and returned to the room to find Max asleep on the rug. I woke him up just enough to sneak a pillow under his head. I grabbed a blanket and placed my pillow next to him. I covered us up with the blanket and rested my head beside his.

He had his eyes closed, so I studied his eyebrows, his forehead, his nose. I was leaving in a few days and then what? No more Max? Back to the city where we supposedly had everything we needed. Get your food in two minutes, like it on Instagram, or discover the latest trend. None of that mattered. Life in the city, where you could get whatever you wanted . . . but barely anything you needed.

Max was special to me, and the thought of leaving him seemed like the most ridiculous thought. Would I come back later in the summer, the fall, the winter? Would he be able to meet me in the winter, or would he be trapped under the ice for all those months?

I ran through all the scenarios that might play out and finally felt secure knowing that Echo Island wasn't that far away. I'm sure my parents would let me stay with Aunt Kat again. I was almost sixteen, after all; I could take the bus or train up to Kingfield and meet Max at the ferry. I reassured myself over and over that this wouldn't end in three days. I finally closed my eyes.

I was drifting in and out of sleep and I felt Max tucking the blanket all the way up to my chin. He tucked it around my shoulders to make sure they wouldn't get cold. I pretended to be asleep, and it felt so nice to have someone watching out for me, tucking me in, and making sure I was warm.

Then he took my hand and held it with his warm hand as I smiled to myself and drifted off to sleep.

Friday, July 15th

I woke up and Max was gone, disappeared again. I sat up, confused, and looked around. But then he came through the door and said nothing at first. He kissed my forehead and then kissed my lips.

"Meet me at Thomas's bar tonight?" he asked.

"To go to the dance?"

"Of course."

"I'll be there at seven," I said. He kissed me again and whispered, "See you tonight."

I watched him from my little window. He walked through the yard and turned to look back at me. He stood and waved. It felt corny, but I sort of started to panic before he looked back up.

I worried for a second that I might not mean much to him, that he'd leave the front yard and not care.

But then it happened. He gazed back at me, from the same spot he did ten years ago. He looked back and waved and it was . . . it was everything to me.

I was dying to know what happened with George and my phone. Plus, I was pretty nervous about that dance. As I've said before, I don't dance much and that mermaid dress?

That dress was a little too form-fitting, but I considered it more of a costume, so I could almost pretend to be someone else. That made it easier to stomach. How bad would the dance really be?

More important was my phone and what happened when George turned over the evidence. I knew what I had to do. I went to his hotel and looked everywhere. I got a sinking feeling when I didn't find him after fifteen minutes of searching.

I was heading to the front desk when I saw him in the lobby with his luggage. I ran over to him and asked what happened.

"Well, I turned it in. The natural resources team was understandably shocked," he said.

"Then what happened?" I asked.

"I followed up this morning and found out that the police have Kyle and Earl in custody. I doubt any of their relatives have the funds to bail them out before any kind of trial. They'll be in jail for a while," he answered.

"That's great news," I said, exhaling with relief. "Thank you so much."

"You did all the hard work. Is it okay if they drop off your phone with your aunt after they're done with it?"

"Sure, that'd be great. A teenager can only go without her phone for so long, right?" I joked.

"Right," he laughed. I looked at all his luggage. "Are you heading back to the city?"

"Not yet. I have some meetings on the mainland. Kingfield awaits. I'm checking into a bed and breakfast over there."

"Oh, good to hear," I said. We both ran out of things to say. "Will you walk me out?" he asked.

I agreed and we headed outside. "Are you coming back

next year, Theresa?" he asked.

"I hope to. I hope to be back before that. I love it up here," I said. The word "love" just came out, but it was true.

When I arrived on the island, I couldn't have imagined myself saying that, but I said it. And I totally meant it. Such a short time on this island, and I was already changed by it.

"We'll have to stay in touch. I might need an intern down in the city. If you're interested, we could chat about that this fall," he said.

"I'd love that. I want to stay involved. I don't know much about what you do, but I'm passionate about the environment," I said.

"I can tell that already," he said. "I better get to the ferry. Here, take my card and stay in touch." He handed me a card from his wallet. "I look forward to hearing from you."

"Thanks, I'll, uh, send you an email, for sure," I said.

"Now, you relax and have fun on this beautiful island. That's what it's here for," he said.

"I will. Promise."

I watched him go, then glanced down at his card and smiled. An internship was going to lead somewhere much better than a pizza shop or coffee shop or any other kind of shop.

The rest of the day flew by and before I knew it, Aunt Kat was zipping me up in the mermaid dress.

"Blue wig, too?" she asked.

"That might help. I can pretend to be someone else, right?" I asked. I tried it on and shook the blue hair around.

"What do you think?" I asked.

"I'd say it's stellar and amazing," she said. She gave me a big hug and started toward the door.

"Need a ride to Max's?" she asked.

"I'm okay, I'll ride the bike," I answered.

"In that dress?"

"Sure, why not?" I said. Aunt Kat just laughed.

"I'll see you on the mainland?" she asked.

"Sure thing," I said.

I biked to Max's a little slower than usual because of the dress. I was getting more anxious about the dance, but I was also excited to see him. As I got closer, I got more and more nervous. This would be a very public date and we were going to be dressed up. I normally don't go to things like this.

When I pulled up to Max's, I found him sitting on the steps of Thomas's bar, waiting for me. He was wearing dark pants, a white dress shirt, and a black tie. He looked like the cutest waiter at a fancy restaurant.

"Wow, Theresa. You're a mermaid," he said with a smile.

"Sort of," I replied nervously. "It has a tail which is so not realistic, I mean, mermaids aren't real, you know. I, uh—"

"We can pretend they're real, right?" he asked.

"Right," I said and we both laughed.

"You look incredible," he said as he stood up from the stairs. "I've never seen you in a dress, it's . . ."

"It's old, I mean vintage. Do you like it?" I asked.

"Very much. I'm worried now."

"Why?" I asked.

"I mean, am I dressed up enough? Is this okay? These are Thomas's clothes. The jacket was a little big, but there's a vest I could try on if you like," he said nervously. He handed the vest to me and I helped him put it on. He turned around, looking like a movie star. I could only gaze at him, speechless.

"What do you think?" he asked.

"Maybe you don't need the jacket. You look great." I wasn't lying; he looked very nice all cleaned up. He even combed his hair, so it was no longer wind-swept. I liked his wild hair, but this was nice, too.

"I have a surprise for you," he said. He held something behind his back. What was he up to? Seeing him all dressed up was enough of a surprise.

"What do you have?" I asked.

"This."

He pulled his hands from behind his back and held one hand out, his palm still closed.

"Okay, open up," I ordered, bossy-like. He opened his palm and there was a simple silver spoon with a chain on it.

"You already had a fork, so I thought—"

"I love it!" I said, cutting him off. He handed it over and I stared down at it.

"Can I wear it tonight?" I asked.

"Do you want to?" he responded. He was back to playing cute, answering questions with a question. This time, it didn't drive me nearly as crazy.

"Of course I want to!" I said and laughed.

"Where's your fork necklace?" he asked.

"Oh, I must have left it at home."

"I love that you wear that. I really do," he said.

"You don't think it's weird? Everyone else does."

"I think it's weird that other people don't do it," he responded.

"How so?" I asked.

"If they had to live all day long with all the plastic forks they've used in their lifetime? If they really thought about it every time they grabbed a new fork, they wouldn't do it. Right?"

"I think you're right. I was trying to lead by example. Start a trend of awareness, but . . ." I stopped myself.

"But what?" he asked.

"It hasn't caught on, I guess," I said. Max was silent for a bit and it started to get awkward for me. I had to break the silence.

"What's up?" I asked.

"You're a very unique and special person, Theresa."

"Me? What about you? You're the unique one between the two of us," I said.

"I'm not really. I'm kind of like the rest of my people. But you? You don't do what other people do."

"I don't know. It's usually not noticed," I said.

"What do you mean?" he asked.

"Exulansis," I said.

"Exulansis?" he asked.

"It's the tendency to give up trying to talk about something because others are unable to relate to it. Sorry, my nerdy ways aren't easy to shake."

"What do you mean?" he asked.

"I mean, if people notice what I'm trying to do, they usually get angry or defensive, so I've almost given up on it. They rarely appreciate what I do. What my friend Brooke and I do."

"I appreciate it," he said.

Who in my life was this direct? I still wasn't used to it. It took me a little while to respond.

"Thank you, Max. I know you do," I said, but I didn't want to be serious yet. We had time for that later.

I wanted to have fun. I didn't want to think of toxic sludge or fracking or plastic or life after high school or life back in the city or my parents or saying goodbye to Max.

I wanted to think only of the present. I had gotten rid of some of my nerdy lifestyle in the last week, and I wasn't ready to get stuck in my over-active brain for our last days together. I made up my mind: I wanted to have fun at an old-fashioned dance hall. I was ready. I wanted to put my reusable spoon necklace on and get moving. I handed the necklace to Max.

"Will you help me?" I turned around and he carefully lifted my hair up. He fastened the necklace, but before I turned around he kissed my neck. It tickled at first and I thought of pulling away. My arms filled with goosebumps, and I tried to rub them away. I didn't want him to notice, so I turned for a kiss.

That kissing world record of almost fifty-nine hours I talked about beating before? That idea was back in my brain again. We kissed for a long time. What's twice as long as fifty-nine hours? That would be close to 120 hours, basically five days. Could I kiss Max for that long? Right then, it felt like I could. But we were interrupted.

"You two are going to be late if you stand in the yard necking all night," Thomas said from across the lawn.

I was pretty mortified. People still say "necking"? Or was it the older crowd who still said it?

Either way: embarrassed!

I wasn't used to kissing guys and getting caught by their grandparents, but we all laughed with each other.

"We're on our way," Max yelled back. He took my hand and we ran toward the trail behind Thomas's bar.

"Goodnight, Thomas!" I yelled back as we ran.

"Stay out of trouble!" he yelled.

"Always!" Max replied.

The sun was going down as we ran, hand in hand. It was a little difficult to be running in a dress, but I did fine. Max looked back at me occasionally to smile and see if I was okay.

I was. I was more than okay.

I felt so happy to be on this wild adventure on the island, in dress-up clothes. His tie blew over his shoulder and flapped in the wind.

I looked down at my shiny mermaid dress. The sunset's rays danced and reflected off it; it lit up the pine needles along the trail. All my necklaces were jingling as I ran.

I noticed more when I was on the island. The colors were brighter, the sounds louder, the birds, the pinecones, the clean smell of dirt, the way Max's hand felt holding mine—not sweaty or clammy, but warm and dry and strong.

We reached the beach and stopped to catch our breath. We looked at each other and laughed. Max sat in the sand on his knees and pulled me down to sit on his lap. He squeezed me really hard and I pretended to protest, but he could've squeezed me forever.

We watched the sun get closer and closer to the horizon. I wished that I had another week on the island. And I wished that the dance hadn't already started. I wanted to slow time and just be with Max.

If he had special powers, why couldn't I have one? The power to freeze time. That's all I wanted. I didn't need to shoot lasers out of my fingers or fly to Mars or read someone's brain. I needed more of *now*.

"Ready?" Max finally asked.

"I guess we can't miss the whole dance, right?"

"Everyone needs to see you in that dress, c'mon."

Max and I stood up and hopped in the canoe he had waiting for us. I sat in the front of the canoe, facing backwards, and Max launched us off the beach. We drifted into open water and Max walked toward me in the boat.

I know you're not supposed to stand in a canoe, but when he glided toward me, the boat didn't even sway. Max knew water, and the idea of him falling out of a boat? Not going to happen.

He whispered, "Now close your eyes and don't open them until I say. Okay?"

"Uh, okay," I said, unsure of what was about to happen. But after successfully diving off a dock from a moving bicycle's handlebars, I knew I was safe.

I peeked a little and saw Max sit down again. He closed his eyes and focused. He started to look up at me, so I quickly shut my eyes before he'd notice.

The boat started moving, and then it really started to move. It went faster and faster. I could feel the wind and the blue hair from my wig was whipping me in the face.

It wasn't scary—it was like a roller coaster. I screamed with excitement; I didn't want it to end. I felt weightless. I could barely feel my body anymore. It was like my soul had traveled out of my body and was floating. The canoe started to slow down and my hair stopped hitting me in the face.

"Okay, open your eyes," Max said. I did. I looked at him and he gave me a little smile. That's when the canoe gently hit the sand of the mainland's beach.

"That was way faster than last time," I said. Max didn't

respond. What was he trying now? His eyes sort of glazed over and he stared at me.

"Max, are you okay?" He didn't answer. "Max. Max!" I said louder. He snapped out of his fog and coughed; he looked really sick.

"I need to . . . the water," he said and leaned over to touch the lake's surface. He almost instantly got the color back in his cheeks. I got scared for a second. I guess our extra-fast canoe trip took a toll on him. I looked around to see if anyone was watching, but we were on a secluded beach.

"Can I do anything to help?" I asked.

"I'll be okay in a minute. Do you mind waiting?" he asked.

"Of course not."

"I'll be back to normal soon. But . . ." he started.

"But what?" I asked.

"Will you, um . . . will you hold my hand?" I didn't say anything. I carefully bumbled toward him in the canoe. I sat down next to him and held his hand. I rested my head on his back and rubbed his hand.

"Are you sure you're okay?" I asked.

"I will be."

"Why did that take so much of your strength?"

"I had to make sure we went fast enough, so that nobody would see us," he answered. I thought about his sacrifice for us to get to the dance quickly. I knew he thought it was important for me, but it wasn't worth it. I squeezed his hand tight.

"I don't like seeing you like this," I finally said.

"I'm sorry," he said.

"No, don't be sorry. It's . . . next time, we won't hurry. Okay?"

"Okay," he answered. He looked at me and smiled. More color had returned to his cheeks and he squeezed my hand back tightly.

"Ready?" he asked.

"I'm ready."

We wandered through the quiet streets of Kingfield toward the dance. We started to hear music and came across the old-fashioned town hall. There were a lot of people talking outside, laughing, telling stories. We watched from a block away for a minute. We needed to observe what we were about to get into.

"Ready?" I finally broke the silence.

"Are you?"

"Not quite, but how bad could it be?" I responded. We crossed the street slowly and made it to the big front door.

Max and I stepped into the town hall nervously. I got a few long stares because of my mermaid dress and blue wig.

"Should I go to the bathroom and take off this wig?" I asked.

"I think it looks great," Max answered. We held hands and without knowing it, I squeezed Max's hand with a strong grip. Max squeezed my hand back and whispered in my ear, "I think you broke my hand."

"What?"

"I'm only joking."

"Sorry!" I lightened up my grip.

We stopped pretty much right when we walked in. Neither one of us was used to spending time in a room full of people. It's safe to say we were both in mild shock.

"What do we do now?" he asked.

"Let's just ease into it. Can we wait here and take it in for a minute?" I asked.

"If you'd like," Max answered.

There were people already dancing, hanging out by the makeshift bar in the back; a band was playing on the small stage.

It looked like a lot of fun, but I didn't know how to get *into* the fun. I'm always on the nerdy-serious side of life and dancing wasn't my thing. If you looked up "I Don't Do Crowds" in the dictionary, my face might appear.

"Maybe we should get some fresh air," I offered.

"We'll be okay. Think of what we might have been doing tonight instead," he said.

"What do you mean?"

"The toxic sludge—we don't have to worry about it anymore. We should be celebrating," he said.

"You're right." I took a deep breath. "Should we get something to drink?" I finally asked.

"Sure," Max answered. We made our way along the side of the dance floor toward the bar. I was super relieved when the bartender turned out to be Aunt Kat.

"Max! Theresa! You finally made it." She came around the bar table and gave us big warm hugs. I could feel some of the tension release when she did.

"Are you ready to dance?" she asked as she returned to the other side of the bar.

"In a little bit," I responded. She gave us some soft drinks and we made our way to the side of the dance floor. I looked back at her and she winked and gave me a "thumb's up" gesture and pointed to Max.

To make things more uncomfortable, I saw my brother Derek flirting with some girls across the room from us. He gave me and my mermaid dress a dirty look and went back to his flirting.

The band finished their song and started a fast-paced one. Out of nowhere a conga line formed. Yes, a conga line. I cringed internally. Max looked confused at the scene that was developing. I tried to smile, but before I knew it, Derek had grabbed my hand, and I had grabbed Max's, and:

We.

Were.

In.

A.

Conga.

Line.

A personal nightmare of mine. I could tell that Derek did it just to make me more uncomfortable and he succeeded. I was mortified.

I was behind Derek and in front of Max. Trapped. I looked back at Max and to my surprise, he laughed with an astonished look on his face. He was so caught up in the moment, staring up at the disco lights and the spectacle of the whole scene. I turned back to Derek and he started blabbing.

"Nice dress," he said as a joke.

"Thank you," I replied, not taking his bait.

"I like your boyfriend," he teased.

"Derek!" I protested.

"What? He's a good dancer."

"You're going to pay for this." I looked back at Max as he continued to look around the room with a huge grin on his face.

I thought, *I need to give in to all of this. At least I was on the dance floor, right?* Max squeezed my waist; I turned back and we both laughed. It was so, so, so corny. I hated to admit it, but I was having a good time. Even Derek looked back and laughed along with me. Maybe being part of a bigger group wasn't such a bad thing. I let go of my attitude and just had fun.

The conga line couldn't last forever, though; the song ended and a slow song started. Derek and some others dispersed, but Max and I stayed, looking at each other. He put his hand around my waist and looked at me.

"I've never done a slow dance, but will you dance with me?" he asked.

"Sure," I said. If I could do that insane conga line, I could do a slow dance. Neither one of us really knew how to do it, but we sort of shuffled along with our instincts and it worked surprisingly well.

We slowly spun around the dance floor and I almost forgot where I was. I felt like I was back in the canoe, floating across the lake. Max's voice broke me out of my daydream.

"How rare that we're both here right now. This night," he said.

"This night?" I asked.

"This night is everything to me," he said and stared directly into my eyes. I didn't know how to respond to his honesty. It was too much. Too face to face.

I pressed my head against his shoulder and squeezed his waist. I looked out the window and up to the sky. There was the blue moon staring back at me. I closed my eyes and the words came out of my mouth almost involuntarily.

"It means everything to me too," I said. I realized I could

say it back, but it was too hard to look at him directly and say it. I meant it like crazy, though.

He might not ever know how much I meant it.

The song had no sign of ending, so we glided across the dance floor. We slowly turned near the side of the town hall, near the windows. I glanced out the window and saw three men at the gas station.

Something about them seemed familiar, but we spun slowly and I couldn't see them. I strained to look and my instinct was right. I knew who they were and it wasn't good. It was a very, very bad sight: I saw George gassing up a boat with Kyle and Earl.

They were supposed to be in jail and George was supposed to be on our side. The instant I understood it was them, I knew I had been majorly fooled. It all came crashing down on me and my feet stopped moving.

George had played me. How could I have not noticed his lies the whole time? Of course he was still working with those guys. How naive could I be? All those nice things he said? Those were just lies. He got me to trust him by pretending he was on my side. And I fell for it. Looking back, I could clearly see when and where he was lying to me. That internship? It was just to butter me up and distract me. I should have trusted my instincts when I first saw George with Kyle and Earl.

I was furious. Max looked at me, but I could only focus on the boat and truck and the barrels of toxic chemicals that were no doubt under the boat's large tarp.

"What's wrong?" Max asked.

"We have to go," I answered. I took Max by the hand and led him outside. We snuck down the side of the town hall to watch those three drive toward the docks.

"Was that those guys, who—" he started to ask.

I cut Max off. "Yes. We have to stop them. George is not who I thought he was."

"It looks like they're going to launch the boat," Max offered.

"Could we follow them?" I asked.

"Yeah, but then what?"

"We stop them!"

"How?" he asked.

"I don't know." I thought about it for a second. "Should we call the police?" I asked, but thought better of it. "I don't think they'll get here on time. Those guys could go anywhere on this huge lake. If we wait for the police, we'll have no chance of finding them."

I was stuck. Frozen.

"Let's get to the canoe. We have to at least try to stop them," he said. We ran through town like thieves, hiding behind buildings and bushes, to make sure George or those guys didn't see us. I couldn't run very well in my mermaid dress, so I stopped us.

"What's wrong?" Max asked.

"I can't run in this dress!" I whispered desperately as I tore off my blue wig. I dropped the string and let the mermaid tail hit the ground, I ripped at the dress.

"Sorry, Aunt Kat. I promise I'll repair this," I said as I transformed her mermaid dress into a mini skirt and continued to run at full speed with Max.

We launched the canoe and paddled along the edge of the great lake. We saw Kyle, Earl, and George on their boat. It was clear they were heading to the island. They wanted to dump the chemicals when everyone was at the dance.

"We'll have to use my powers to get to Echo Island before them," Max offered.

"But then you'll be weak again, won't you be?"

"I'll have time to heal once we get there," he replied. He placed his hands in the water and I closed my eyes. My mind was racing with ideas. We made record time back to the island, but this time it wasn't fun. It was dark out and we were full of panic.

Max must've been distracted, because instead of gently gliding to shore, we hit the beach with a hard thud. I held on tight, but he was so weak that his body flew out of the canoe and onto the beach. I ran to him to make sure he was okay. He was barely moving.

"The water," he whispered urgently.

I tried to pick him up to his feet, but he couldn't stand, so I dragged him to the edge of the beach and placed his hands in the lake. I scooped up a handful of water and washed the mud off his face. He wasn't responding and I got really scared.

I focused my sight along the horizon and saw the lights from George's boat in the distance, just minutes away. Max woke up and slowly got better. He eventually took off his shoes, and stood in the water.

"I'm okay," he finally said. I hugged him, but got more and more nervous the closer the boat came.

"What are we going to do?" I asked.

"I don't know," Max answered.

"Let's get to a spot where they won't see us," I offered. We snuck along the shore and hid behind some large rocks. They were still pretty far away, but we could hear them arguing. Maybe their arguing was a good sign for us? Did George have a change of heart? Was he going to turn the two brothers over to the police?

Then we heard the unmistakable sounds of six gun shots and two large splashes. Max looked back at me with a grave expression. I gasped, but he covered my mouth with his hands.

We both knew that something was terribly wrong. Did George have a plan to get rid of Kyle and Earl? Or did those two guys shoot him?

This was about more than pollution; it was likely about murder. A new thought popped into my head: *Were we going to make it out of this alive?*

"I think we'll need more help," Max said.

"What do you mean? Your Grandfather Tibor?"

"We don't want him involved right now. He'd be too angry," Max replied and added, "Lily is on her way to help. I could feel her presence when I touched the water. She sensed that I was in trouble."

"Can she help us?" I asked.

"Yes, but we need more than Lily. We need the police or Thomas or someone to help. Kat's Club isn't far. Could you run and call the police?" Max asked. This idea made some sense, but he acted weird about asking me. I couldn't tell what was going on. I was so confused. He wasn't acting like himself.

"Do you think that's a good idea?" I asked.

"Theresa, we don't have much time," he responded.

"I don't want to leave you here," I said.

"I'll be fine, don't worry," he said. I looked at him and he looked toward the lake.

"Please, go!" he said. He wouldn't look me in the eye and I got so frustrated and confused that I took off running.

I ran through the woods for a few minutes, thinking I would cry at any second. What was really going on?

I stopped to catch my breath. I clutched the spoon necklace and realized it: Max didn't need the police; he needed me to be out of harm's way. That was an excuse to get me away from the danger. I wasn't about to leave for that reason. I turned around and sprinted back. I got closer to shore and slowly crept up to a safe place behind a rock to watch the scene.

George was still in the boat near shore, but Earl and Kyle were nowhere to be seen. He must have been the one doing all the shooting. Were they dead? Either way, they were gone.

He dragged a barrel to the edge of the boat and started dumping the toxic sludge, but it wasn't hitting the water—the sludge was circling back up into the barrel, like a waterfall or fountain going upwards and in a cycle.

I looked down and saw Max on the shore holding his hand out, his eyes closed tight. He was controlling whatever toxic liquid was in the barrel, preventing it from hitting the water's surface.

George angrily pulled the barrel upright and took something from his pocket. I moved in to see if I could help Max, but then I heard it.

Another gunshot.

Then another one.

I scrambled to see what had happened. I crouched down and saw Max lying on the beach, with two gun shot wounds: one to his leg and one to his shoulder.

He looked up to me and held his hand toward me, motioning me to stay where I was. George tied the boat to the dock and ran toward Max. I did the same, but after a second of moving, my body froze. Max was using the last of his powers to stop me from taking one more step. I was out of sight and safe, but unable to help.

Max was controlling all the water in my body; I was frozen in my tracks. It was terrifying. I thought my heart would beat right out of my body, it was beating so fast.

I saw George aim his gun at Max again, but the second he fired it, a wall of water rose up from the lake and surrounded Max, protecting him from the bullets. I could barely move my eyes, but I was able to make out Lily.

She stood near the woods, with both hands up. She held the water shield in place as George fired shot after shot. He must've run out of bullets because the shooting stopped.

Lily's water shield evaporated; she fell to her knees and collapsed. George looked right up at her. He looked back at Max, but Max wasn't moving.

Lily struggled to get to her feet, but fell again. George darted toward her. I was able to move my eyes and I focused down on my hands. My fingers twitched. Whatever spell Max had put on me to stop me from moving, it was about to wear off. My legs gave way and I fell to the ground. I could feel my arms and legs come back to life.

George reached Lily and scooped her off the ground. He looked around and hauled Lily onto the boat. He drove the boat down the shore and completely out of sight.

I managed to crawl toward Max, and eventually I was able to get to my feet. I saw the lights of George's boat go down the island, but not toward the mainland. Where was George taking Lily if he was staying near the island?

By the time I got to Max, he had made his way to the water's edge. He had his index finger in the water, but he wasn't moving. I pulled him closer to the water and flipped his body over.

"Max. Max!" I screamed. He still didn't move. I looked down the side of the island and saw George's boat disappear completely. I held Max tight and whispered in his ear, "Please. Max. Wake up."

"Theresa," he finally whispered.

"Yeah."

"You're not safe with me."

"What?"

"Tibor. He knows what's happening now; he can sense it in the water. He knows that Lily and I are in trouble."

"Where is he?" I asked.

"He's far away, but can get here very fast. If we move away from the shore, it will be harder for him to find us," he said.

"How do you feel?" I asked. Max seemed strong enough to sit up.

"I need to rest for another minute, then we can go."

"Where?" I asked.

"Maybe we can hide with Thomas. I don't want your aunt to get involved. There's no telling what Tibor might do," he said.

"What about Lily?" I asked. "We need to help her."

"It's too dangerous right now—we won't be able to find her in the dark. Tibor will be able to locate us if I use more of my powers, then you'll be in danger," he said.

"What are we going to do?" I asked.

"I don't know." We stared at each other, not knowing what else to say. He reached over and held my hand. We were silent for a minute.

"We need to get away from the water now," Max said. We stood up and started down a woodsy trail away from the beach.

It was really dark out, but the moon lit up our trail.

We finally made it back to Thomas's house, but it was completely dark. We decided it was best to not wake him up, so we snuck through the house and made it to Max's room.

"I feel bad, with Lily out there," I said.

"We have to rest. We won't do Lily any good right now. We'll look for her first thing in the morning."

"Are you sure?"

"I know. I can sense that she's weak, but she's not in danger right now. I don't want to risk Tibor finding you," Max said.

I sat on the bed, defeated. Max sat next to me and gave me a hug. I rested my head on his shoulder.

"Your clothes are soaking wet," I said.

"I know. I'm going to get some dry clothes, okay?"

"Of course." Max left the room. I sat alone on the bed, still in my destroyed mermaid dress and blue shoes. I felt helpless and hopeless and small.

We were so happy and carefree at the dance, and now things were so different, so dark and scary. Two men were at the bottom of the lake. Max and I almost lost our lives, and now Lily was with a killer—George.

How had I let myself be fooled by him? I was smart enough to get good grades in chemistry, but I couldn't see a scam artist when he was right in front of me. I covered my face with my hands and exhaled.

I wanted to go back to last week, when all I worried about was hauling garbage to hang on Mooshy. That seemed so far away from where I was.

He returned and stood at the door. I took my hands down to look at him. He looked down at the clothes he had for me.

"Are you okay?" he asked.

"I think so," I said and Max handed me a large T-shirt.

"This is Thomas's. Will it work to sleep in?"

"I don't know how I'll be able to sleep, I'm so worried about Lily," I said as I took the T-shirt from him.

I was about to leave the room and change into the shirt, but then I remembered that he'd already seen me in a bathing suit. What difference is a bra and underwear?

"I'll be right back," Max offered.

"No, it's okay," I said and Max sat down on the edge of the bed. I stripped out of the dress and into the shirt. When my head popped out of the shirt, I looked to Max. True to his gentleman nature, he had his back turned to give me privacy.

"I can help you sleep if you'd like," he said.

"You can do that?" I asked.

"Yeah, if you want. I can help put your mind at rest." I sat down next to him.

"I have so many thoughts running around in my brain right now. I think I might need your help," I said.

"Okay. Let's go to sleep," Max said. He put his warm, dry hand on my forehead and I could instantly feel the energy of his body. I looked at him and swallowed a lump in my throat and closed my eyes.

"Lily will be okay. We're going to find her," he said. I normally take off my fork necklace at night, but now it was a spoon necklace—a little less dangerous to sleep with than a fork. I kept it on, reached up, and held it tight.

"Goodnight, Max."

"Goodnight, Theresa."

Saturday, July 16th

I woke up in Max's bed alone, but extremely rested. Whatever he did to the water in my brain really worked. The events of the previous night came back to me in a flurry. I rushed to put my dress back on, but it didn't seem practical. I kept the T-shirt on, found pajama bottoms and a hoodie to wear.

I searched the house, but couldn't find Max or Thomas. Confused, I flung open the front door to find snow.

Snow? Again? This time, there was a ton on the ground. I saw a few footsteps that led to the trail behind Thomas's house. Thomas's truck was gone, so the footsteps must've been Max's.

I grabbed one of Thomas's puffy vests and ran out the door and down the trail. The footsteps were messy, as if Max had been running. My eyes widened in alarm and the adrenaline kicked in. My suspicions were confirmed as I got closer to the water's edge.

I could hear Max arguing with someone in a tone I'd never heard before. When I made it to the shore, I noticed that the lake was frozen over. Max was far away on the ice, so it was hard to tell who he was with. I jumped on the ice and made my way closer to them.

It was an older man with wild silver hair and he was half out of the water, where the ice hadn't formed yet. I thought that it must have been his grandfather, Tibor.

He was holding a large wood stick, sort of like a spear; it was all twisted and made out of tree roots but with sharp points. The moment Tibor saw me, he glared intensely at me and vanished under the water. Ice formed where Tibor had been and I had no doubt that he was making all the ice and snow happen.

I ran toward Max and he sprinted toward me, waving his hands.

"No, Theresa! Turn back!" he hollered.

"What's happening?"

"It's too dangerous here! Go back!" he yelled.

The wind swept up really fast and it snowed even harder. I could barely believe what was happening. Max and I were getting closer and closer. Even though he didn't want me on the ice, I kept running toward him.

"Theresa!" he screamed as he held his hand up to get me to stop. He looked so worried, but I wanted to be there.

Max looked around and he must've sensed something in the ice. He slid to a stop and looked me in the eye, and with his hand held out to me, the ice that circled him melted away instantly and he fell into the water.

The second he went under the surface, the ice froze over again. I never stopped running and I quickly arrived to the spot he fell through. I slid to my knees and pounded on the ice, but I couldn't find Max under the surface.

"Max!" I screamed with tears in my eyes as I banged on the ice. Nothing happened, I didn't even make the smallest crack in the ice. I kept banging and banging, but still nothing happened.

I finally stopped and wiped away the snow to see him better. He stared up at me, but neither of us could say anything. He pressed his hand against the ice and I did the same thing.

"No," I said quietly, defeated and confused. Then, in a flash, Max was swept away by an underwater current. I ran in the direction he was moving under the ice, but soon lost track of him.

I felt like falling to my knees to sob, but my instinct for survival kicked in. I looked all around me. The air changed all around me. The sun came out and the snow stopped almost instantly. I heard the ice crack—loud and deep sounds like I'd never experienced before.

I didn't have time to think, I had to run. I ran toward land as fast as I could.

The ice beneath me opened and I fell in. My limbs stung from the freezing cold water and my legs and arms went numb pretty fast. I swam the best I could to shore. I had to battle huge ice chunks the whole way. But the ice was melting and the air temperature of the late summer returned to its full force.

By the time I had clawed my way to shore, most of the ice was gone. I shivered and turned back to see if there was a sign of anyone.

Max must've already been miles away and Tibor's control of the water was no longer a force.

Was I the only one to witness this? Did the snow and ice only affect where Max and I were? This part of the island was so remote, that was a possibility.

I looked around for a helping hand from anyone, but I was alone. Max was gone. Was he gone for good? How was I going to find Lily?

I knew I needed to get warm first. I ran back to Thomas's house and changed into some dry clothes and warmed up. I called Aunt Kat and lied to her, told her everything was fine.

"Are you sure? You don't sound like everything is fine," she said.

"I'm good, really. I'm a little sad because my time on the island is coming to an end." That part wasn't a lie.

We talked a little more about the dance and why I wasn't there longer. I didn't want her to get involved and be put in danger, so I kept making up stories. I tried to get off the phone as soon as possible because I needed to find Lily.

Thomas never came back from his errands, so I set off on my bike alone. But where would George have taken Lily? He was checked out of the hotel, and you can't exactly smuggle a kidnapped girl into your room.

I biked like crazy around the island. It was a relatively small place, but there were so many woodsy areas that it seemed impossible to find Lily. What was I looking for? I wouldn't be able to see George's boat from the road, but I kept going anyway. What else could I do?

I made it to the "wealthier" side of the island, where most people had big modern lake homes. Things seemed to be getting more and more hopeless.

A few clouds rolled in fast, followed by a quick rain. *Soaked again*, I thought. I had to keep going; Lily was more important than having wet clothes.

I stopped in my tracks when I noticed a dry line on the pavement. The width of a sidewalk—a line that the rain never hit. It was like when Max made us a bubble of air to protect us from the rain. Was he making this? It must've been him—who else could it have been?

I stood in the dry section of the street and looked around with wonder. I noticed that the chunk of dryness went to a trail down a gravel road and into the woods. *A secret hint from Max?*

I dumped my bike and ran toward the woods. The dry path took me to another path. I ran down it and all the rain stopped completely. I knew then that I was on the right track.

I made it to a secluded rocky beach near a dock with George's boat tied to it! I looked up the stairs that ran up to an expensive house. I crept up toward it and it looked like the lock on the fence's gate was smashed open. This was the place, George's temporary hideout.

What was his next move? He had already killed two men and broken into an empty luxury vacation house. He was capable of anything. I had no clue what to do.

I snuck around the tall fence and peered through the cracks. At first, I couldn't see much, but I finally saw George pacing back and forth in the living room. He was smoking a cigarette in the house, but eventually he stomped out to the pool and stared into the deep end.

He threw his cigarette in the pool and lit another one. He stormed out of the gate and down the sidewalk toward the lake.

This was my small window of time to find Lily. I scrambled over the fence and ran through the house. She was nowhere to be found inside. My heart was racing like crazy. George was moments away from possibly discovering me.

I peeked out the kitchen window and saw him sitting on

the stairs that led to the dock. I was still safe. I ran out to the patio and noticed something out of the corner of my eye, in the pool. I looked closer and discovered that it was Lily.

She was at the bottom of the deep end, chained to a car tire. She looked up at me, but didn't move. The look on her face was so sad and hopeless. I ran toward the edge of the pool and she swam slowly up to me.

"Are you okay?" I whispered urgently.

"I've been poisoned," she answered.

"How? Don't you get strength from the water?"

"George found out that the chlorine from the pool made me weak, so he dumped a lot in the pool and left me here. I don't have the strength to drag this tire out of the pool."

"We have to get you out of here. I'll get something to cut the chain."

"Wait!" Lily whispered.

"What?"

"I saw my grandfather yesterday, before I found you and Max."

"What happened?" I asked.

"He knows something is happening. If those chemicals make it into the lake, he will freeze the entire lake to stop the chemicals from going anywhere," she said.

"Okay, that's a good thing. Right?" I asked.

"He'll make the temperature so low that . . ." I figured out what she was saying and finished her sentence.

"Everyone on the island will freeze to death," I said.

"Yes," she said.

I ran to the fence and saw that George was still by the dock. I dove in the pool and hauled the tire to the surface and helped Lily out of the pool.

I put her arm around me, picked up the tire, and hauled us all to the garage. We looked for a bolt cutter, but couldn't find one. We found a tiny saw and I started cutting the chain. I was halfway through, but it was taking forever. I peeked up for any sight of George. I didn't spot him in the house or near the pool, so I kept cutting and cutting.

I was finally able to cut through the chain and free Lily. We turned to sneak out of the garage and found George standing before us, blocking our escape. And he had his gun pointed directly at us.

"Let's go. Now," he said.

I helped Lily to her feet and George ordered us to the side of the pool. He handed me a bottle of chlorine.

"Dump this on her."

"No!" I protested.

"Do it!" he said and pointed the gun at me. I looked down at Lily's big trusting eyes. She stared straight into my heart, the same way Max did.

"It's okay, Theresa," she said.

"I can't," I said with tears forming in my eyes. "Please don't make me do this."

"Do it," George said and shoved me in the back with his gun. I picked up the chlorine and started to cry, but I wiped away my tears. I didn't want to give George any satisfaction.

"I'm so sorry, Lily," I whispered.

"I know," Lily said as she closed her eyes.

"C'mon! Do it!" George ordered.

I dumped a quarter of the bottle on her. It was torture for me, not to mention for Lily. How did it get to this point? This was all my fault. I dragged Max and Lily into this, but I didn't have to pay for my actions. They did. Lily collapsed onto the deck; she looked so lifeless and pale.

"More!" George barked at me.

"No, that's enough."

"I'll say when it's enough," he said with a vicious tone. I poured more, but then I lost my mind for a second. I didn't care what happened to me. I turned to George, held the bottle up, and dropped it to the ground with defiance.

"You stupid little girl, that was your last mistake. Pick her up and drag her to the boat."

He motioned for us to move down to the boat. It wasn't easy getting Lily moving; she was barely alive.

George managed to get her on the boat while pointing his gun at me. He kept staring back at me to make sure I wasn't up to anything.

"You! Get in the boat too," he ordered. I sat down next to the barrels of toxic chemicals.

I watched as Lily collapsed at the front of the boat. George ordered me to sit across from him as he started the boat and took off across the lake.

What was going to happen? No matter what, it was sure to be messy. There was no easy solution to any of this. I looked up to the sky for a sign from Max, but I noticed nothing.

I scanned the horizon as we zipped across the water. We were getting really close to the mainland, but I could tell George was looking for a covert spot to dock the boat. He traveled parallel to the coastline. I was hoping to see Max standing on a rock with a magical wave to take George and his stupid gun out of this equation, but there was no Max.

We passed a rocky area of the mainland and something caught my eye—a gigantic elk. Was it the real Mooshy staring at us?

"What?" I whispered to myself in awe. George followed my eye line to see the elk too. We were both dumbstruck and distracted by the scene of this regal animal that seemed to be telling us something.

I thought of Mooshy, the statue. How I had wanted to make a statement against pollution with his help. Now, where was I? I had failed Mooshy and this real-life elk, who seemed to look right into my heart. If this was the real Mooshy, he would have said, "You've failed us."

The elk turned and moved out of sight. Every minute that passed, the worse I felt. I wanted to help Lily somehow, but I knew there was nothing I could do. I noticed George's eyes on me. He kept staring and finally laughed.

"What's that?" he asked and pointed at the spoon necklace that Max gave me.

"My necklace," I said.

"You're going to save the world with a stupid fork and spoon?" He reached over and yanked it off my neck.

"Good luck," he added. I looked over to him, but I had nothing left to say. He was a murderer and a polluter and a torturer.

I looked down at my feet in a daze. The wind was causing my hair to hit me in the face over and over.

I recognized then that I probably wasn't going to ever make it back to the mainland, the island, or the city. I thought to myself, *This really might be it for me. My last day on the planet.*

If George succeeded, Aunt Kat, Derek, Thomas, and everyone on the island wouldn't survive the freeze that Tibor would bring. I wouldn't survive it either. I was too sad and scared to cry. Too shocked.

I glanced over at Lily's body for any sign of something positive, but there was nothing. Nobody knew where we were and barrels of toxic chemicals were about to be dumped into this beautiful lake.

George looked down at my necklace and threw it into the lake with disdain.

"I used to be like you. I used to want to save everything. Then I finally figured out that the train had already left the station. It's the end of the world; we can't stop it now." He looked at me, wanting a shocked reaction. I wouldn't give him that. He didn't deserve that, but he kept talking anyway.

"Why not make some money and be comfortable while I'm on this planet? Fundamentally, I'm on your side, Theresa," he added.

I wanted him to shut up so bad. I wanted off that boat. I wanted to be anywhere else. George moved closer to me and tucked my wild hair behind my ear.

"A pretty girl shouldn't worry about the world so much," he said.

I was beyond angry, but I was feeling so many emotions that it sort of scrambled my brain and I could barely move. I was beyond trying to argue. It was all about survival at that point, and I wasn't going to do anything but focus on my first chance to be free and to stay alive.

"You'd look a lot better if you'd smile. Would that kill you?" he asked.

I was numb to anything that came out of his mouth. I knew he had a gun and I couldn't give him the speech he really deserved.

Then it happened. Something that almost made me truly

smile inside. I was too afraid to believe it at first, but there was no denying it.

It was hail. Crazy big hail, and more of it was falling with each second. It hit the boat with brutal force, cracking the windshield and denting the boat everywhere. George was getting pelted by it, but the hail never touched Lily or me.

"Max," I whispered to myself.

I knew that he had found us! My heart felt like it would explode. When I saw the look on George's face, I realized I had a chance to live. George was completely dumbfounded.

"What the hell?" he shouted as he hunched over and tried to protect his head. I took his distraction as my window of opportunity and went for it with two tons of adrenaline driving me.

I grabbed the fire extinguisher and clocked him across the face with all the strength I had. He flew to the back of the boat and landed on the floor. He held his face, blood shooting out of his mouth as he yelled at me.

"You rotten bitch!"

"Don't you forget it!" I screamed back without even knowing what I was saying. I yanked on the steering wheel of the boat, pulling it to one side as hard as I could. The basic physics of this action? I made the boat flip, which was my goal.

What I had planned to do next? I had no idea. We all flew overboard, but as I was literally upside-down in the air, time felt like it moved into extreme slow motion and in this slow motion, I saw Max.

He was swimming in the middle of a large wave he must have created. He looked like a dolphin inside an ocean breaker. The wave was thin at the top, and I could see him clearly in it. Time practically stopped, our eyes locked, and everything seemed to float.

Waves.

Hail.

Barrels of chemicals.

Lily.

George.

and Max . . .

The boat had flipped and everything was up in the air, seeming to float slowly, like astronauts in space.

From my mid-air cartwheel, I held my hand out for Max and he held his hand out for me, but we were too far away to touch. That moment of our hands extending toward each other seemed to last, frozen in time, five seconds or more.

I saw concern in Max's face, but I also saw something else. His eyes told me everything. I could feel his voice in my head. It was like he was whispering to me in my little attic room.

"You're so brave and you've done a very courageous thing. We've already won this fight. We've won because we both care so much about what's right. We're so close, don't give up. Take a deep breath now and fight like crazy to swim to the surface."

Just then, I saw Max's hand pierce through the wave and into the open air. He was reaching for me, reaching and reaching.

And then everything went completely dark.

When I finally woke up, I was on shore, lying in the soft beach sand. I wasn't sore, and I didn't have a single drop of water to cough up.

Had this all been a dream? Was I asleep?

There seemed to be no sound registering in my ears and I was so confused that I barely registered that a police officer was standing right in front of me, asking questions, but I couldn't hear him. I finally uttered, "I'm fine. I'm fine," but he didn't go away.

I looked around and saw George. A team of medics was loading him into an ambulance. I noticed he was handcuffed to the gurney, so I exhaled with relief.

More police officers were on site, staring at the barrels of chemicals that were lined up on shore. I stood up and scanned the scene, but there was no sign of Max or Lily or Tibor.

The boat was turned upright and was sitting calmly in the water. I wandered around, trying to make sense of everything. I wanted to talk to Max to see what happened. Were they all safe? I could barely make out the sound of my name.

"Theresa! Theresa!" Aunt Kat hollered as she and Derek ran toward me. My hearing slowly started to come back as she hugged me. Even Derek hugged me. They were saying things, but none of it was registering, I was so confused. I didn't know what to feel. I was so happy to be safe on solid land and so happy to see them that my tears started on their own.

Sunday, July 17th

I didn't see Max or Lily anymore that Saturday. Aunt Kat was so concerned that she wanted me home and in bed so she could keep an eye on my recovery. I had a cut on my forehead, but I felt 100 percent fine. There wasn't much to recover from.

Okay, maybe I was 90 percent fine. The missing 10 percent was taken up by my worries for Max and Lily.

They must have cleaned up the entire mess after the boat accident, so I'm sure they were okay, but I had to find out for myself. I wanted to see them with my own eyes.

Around midnight, I snuck out of the house and hopped on my bike for one last ride. With all the action, I forgot that Sunday was *the* day. My last day. And it was after midnight, so my last day had officially arrived.

My parents would be getting off that ferry in about nine hours and then we would be heading back to the city.

I biked past Mooshy the Elk, but didn't see any trash to offer up to him. He still looked as noble as the first time I saw him. But was he proud of me for what I had done?

Nobody was around, so I saluted him as if he were my

general or something. I laughed to myself a little, but as I got closer to Max's house, my heart sank.

There were no lights on and Thomas's bar was closed. I walked toward the house and leaned my bike quietly against a tree. It was too late to knock, so I played detective for one last time. I moved toward the windows and glanced in and saw Thomas sleeping peacefully on the couch.

I found Max's room, but the bed was empty. Of course it was empty; he mostly slept in the water. I took off down the trail behind Thomas's bar and made my way to the water. With nobody in sight, I started to get scared. I reached down and touched the water, hoping Max would sense that I was there. I heard a branch snap and turned quickly, but it was nothing. Maybe a rabbit or deer. It was a chilly, crisp night, so I rubbed my arms to stay warm and zipped my jacket up tight.

My hand's presence in the water didn't do anything to bring Max back to me. *Where could he be?* I thought. *Was I about to leave the island without seeing him again?* I felt sick to my stomach at the thought of that, but there was nothing to do but go back to Aunt Kat's.

I slept like a rock and woke up to voices and the smell of pancakes and all things that make up a good morning, but it wasn't a good morning. I was still restless.

The voices belonged to my parents, so I went down to be greeted with big hugs. We weren't a family of frequent hugs, so this was a big deal for them and for me. Their Midwest iciness had melted a little, and I have to admit, I liked the hugs. The whole scientifically proven stress-relieving factor and all ... Oh whatever, it was nice to get all the hugs. Period.

I had been through so much and with so many concerns for Max and Lily still lingering, I really needed a hug.

"We heard what happened. Are you sure you're okay?" my mom asked.

My dad chimed in too. "Who's this George guy? How long will he be in jail? Do you have to testify against him?"

I answered all their questions the best I could and made my way to the table. Saving the environment and late-night bicycling can make a teenager pretty hungry.

We all sat down as my mom and dad served breakfast. Aunt Kat tried to protest and help out, but they wouldn't allow it. The sun was streaming in and my slippers were so cozy and we were all together and getting along.

Even Derek was nice. He brought me my fork necklace to eat breakfast with.

"Here's your, uh . . . fork. You know, for breakfast," he said. But I knew it took the world for him to be that nice to me.

I thought, *Is this how other families are all the time? Could we be this caring more often?*

After breakfast we hung out on the front porch, not doing much at all.

"Ready for a swim on the point?" my mom asked.

"Huh?"

My mom hadn't been an outdoorsy person in years, but the next thing I knew I was next to her on the beach. She and I were done swimming, but Aunt Kat, Derek, and my dad swam longer in the beautiful lake. She added some shampoo to her hair and lathered it up.

"Wait, Mom," I protested.

"Got it covered." She handed me the shampoo bottle and I scanned its ingredients: all natural and biodegradable.

"Huh," I said to myself, surprised.

"You didn't think I knew what shampoo to use, did you?"

"Well, I just wanted to make sure," I answered.

I started sudsing up my own hair. It felt so great to be washing my hair out in the fresh air, feeling toasty in the warm sun. The perfect blend of warm and cool.

"Your Aunt Katherine taught me a lot when we were younger, lessons I haven't forgotten," my mom added. Maybe she wasn't 100 percent like the other massive consumers of all things disposable. I looked at her and smiled and studied her.

"What? Do I have something on my face?" She must have noticed me staring at her.

"No," I laughed. "It's just, you're not exactly a big environmentalist."

"I'm getting better. It must be all those facts you knock me over the head with day after day!" she joked.

"Mom!" I protested.

She looked around and took in the view of the lake. "I forgot how much you don't need when you're on this island," she said.

"What do you mean?" I asked.

"When you've got a view like this, you don't need all that material stuff, do you?"

"Don't need a hundred plastic storage bins?" I joked.

"Hey!" she said and pinched my elbow playfully. I didn't want to get too gushy, so I handed her the bucket of water.

"Sure you're ready to get soaked? It's really cold," she asked.

"I'm ready."

She hoisted up the bucket of water and dumped it over

my head. I screamed with shock from the cold water. I shook my head and did a little dance to warm up. I wiped my eyes with a towel and opened them up, suds-free. Then I saw a blurry figure approaching us. I squinted to see who it was.

It was Max.

He was on the beach walking directly toward us. And I was looking like a drowned rat. I had a few seconds to pull myself together, but I guess I didn't really care. I was so happy to see Max alive and healthy.

My mom must have noticed me staring at Max. He was close enough for us to see his smile, but far enough away that he couldn't hear us.

"Who's that giving you that gigantic smile?" she asked.

"That's Max."

"He appeared out of nowhere. Is he magic?" she asked. She couldn't have imagined what she was really asking me.

"Well, yeah. A little," I said.

"I thought you didn't believe in magic."

"I don't."

"You used to say that science was magic without the lies."

"Did I say that?" I asked.

"And I'd respond by saying, 'Magic is science that you don't understand yet,'" she answered.

After my short time on the island. All the adventure. All the stuff I'd never done, the stuff I would have never believed. The danger, the excitement, the kissing, the daring . . . the magic—I knew my mom was right, but I was still her daughter, so I couldn't let her get away with being right that easily.

"Did you read that saying on an engraved rock in the Echo Island gift shop?" I teased.

I held up her bucket of water and threatened to soak her with it. She laughed through her protests, but before long, Max was standing before us and I had to pretend to be civilized.

"Max, I'd like you to meet my mom."

Max approached her and she looked him up and down. I could tell she was impressed.

"Out for a swim, Max?" she asked.

"Yep," he answered.

We had a little small talk. Max was very charming and polite. He didn't say much, but my mom seemed impressed.

We ran out of things to say and we all stood awkwardly for a few seconds. My mom finally broke the silence by picking up her bucket and saying, "Time to rinse!"

She marched away, rinsed off her hair with a bucket, and went back into the water.

I looked into Max's eyes. I was so relieved and so happy and so EVERYTHING ALL AT ONCE.

But I didn't look him in the eye for very long because I knew what was coming—we had to say our goodbyes.

"Are you okay?" I finally asked.

"I'm okay. Are you?"

"Yesterday was scary, but I'm good," I answered.

"It was," he said.

"Lily? Is she okay?"

"Yeah, she's 100 percent good," he replied. I exhaled with relief. Max moved his foot in the sand. "Could I give you a hug?" he asked.

I glanced around nervously, not wanting my parents or Derek to see, but before I looked back at Max, he had his arms around me. He squeezed me so tight.

It all came crashing down on me: everything we had been through and the fact that I was leaving that day. A quick tear fell from my face, but I tried to cover it up with a laugh.

"Sure you're okay?" he asked.

"I'm great," I said, but I wasn't sure how I really felt. Something felt off.

I heard my brother whistle at us, so Max and I broke our embrace. We waved to Derek and Aunt Kat and my parents as they walked away.

"Don't be too long!" my dad yelled back at us. We watched them stroll back toward Aunt Kat's and we sat down in the sand.

I had a sudden urge to be mean to Max. I figured out what was off, and that was the fact that I had to leave the island.

If we got in a huge fight, it'd be easier to leave him on this sad stupid beach. Okay, the beach wasn't stupid. The whole leaving Max thing was stupid.

I didn't comprehend it completely at the time, but I was experiencing Mauerbauertraurigkeit.

A long fancy German word that means the inexplicable urge to push people away, even close friends who you really like.

Max was more than a close friend, but he wasn't really my boyfriend. In many ways, he felt like more than a boyfriend even though we'd only known each other for barely two weeks.

Mauerbauertraurigkeit? All my weird and favorite scientific words? I suddenly didn't care about them. I didn't want to find fancy words anymore; I didn't want to have this feeling anymore. This long, hard-to-pronounce word was just a complicated way to say that everything sucked and I didn't know what to do.

"I have to go," I said abruptly.

"I should too. I have to help Thomas at the bar." I expected Max to protest a little, so this only fueled my urge to be mean to him.

"Okay, bye. This is stupid," I said coldly.

"What is?"

"All of this. Saying goodbye. You. Me." I stormed away.

"Wait up! Theresa!" he hollered for me. I turned to face him.

"Can I have a hug goodbye?" he asked.

"We already hugged," I said and continued to walk. He followed.

"Theresa, wait!" I didn't stop and I didn't turn around. I didn't want him to see me about to bawl my eyes out like a baby. What was I supposed to say? *See you next summer?* What would be more cliché than that?

I didn't stop until I was in the woods. I hid behind a tree and looked for Max. He wasn't hard to find. He hadn't moved at all. He searched for me to come back, but then he looked down at the sand. He turned and walked toward the water.

The right thing to do was to run back to him and say how stupid I had acted and that nothing was making sense and that I already missed him. All that honest stuff wasn't my style, so I ran away.

Max took one last glance for me with such a sad expression that it hurt me. Like, it was practically physically painful. I could feel it in my throat and in my arms and in my chest. I know all the science behind why my body was doing what it was doing, but that didn't help. The feeling still just plain sucked.

Everyone was packing for the ferry when I got back to Aunt Kat's. I ran up to the attic room and threw everything in my suitcase. It's easy to pack when you're going home. You know that everything has to go. There are no other decisions to make. The vacation was over. Everything was ending.

I sighed heavily to myself and stared at the little door that led to the secret attic room. Maybe if I crawled in, I'd see Max through the little window. He might have a bird he could release to show me that everything was going to be okay.

I nervously opened the door and went in. I crept slowly toward the window and looked out. There was no Max.

I picked a few pillows up and a small piece of white birch bark dropped to the floor. It was the note from Max. The one that he had tied to a tree with a piece of red yarn about a week ago.

"You're almost there. —Max."

I was so happy that I had kept that note. I smiled to myself and put it in my pocket.

I closed the attic's secret door and rested my forehead against it and exhaled.

"Theresa, time to go," Aunt Kat yelled up the stairs. I stopped in the doorway and took one last look around the room. I hadn't even slept in this room for two weeks, but it seemed like months. I had experienced more emotions in this room and on this island than I had in years back in the city.

I couldn't live this fantasy forever. It was time to go back home. I brushed the hair out of my face and left the room.

The next thing I knew, Aunt Kat was dropping us off at the dock near the ferry.

"I'm so proud of you," she said as she hugged me. "And if you don't come back to waiting tables soon, I'll have to hire someone to replace you," she joked.

"Thanks, Aunt Kat. You're awesome," I said.

"I know," she said and we both laughed.

We hopped on the ferry and it eventually left the dock. My mom tried to talk to me about Max, but gave up her questions after all my simple "yes" and "no" answers.

I didn't know what to feel and I certainly didn't want to talk it out with my mom. She didn't follow me when I wandered to the back of the ferry.

I waved to Aunt Kat and noticed that two figures joined her. It was Lily and Thomas. They both gave me huge goodbye waves. I was sad I didn't get to say goodbye, but the waving from the dock was perfect. I was a little relieved not to do it face to face; I was already experiencing so many emotions.

Everyone else climbed up to the second-level deck to get the best view from the front. The ferry pulled farther away from the island and I struggled to get one last look at Echo Island's mascot, my friend, Mooshy the Elk.

I saw his legs and antlers, but the trees got in the way of me seeing his face. I wanted to see what kind of signal he'd send me this time. Would his eyes tell me to jump off the ferry and give Max one last kiss? Or would he tell me not to worry, that I'd be back on the island before I knew it?

Without an answer from Mooshy, I still felt that I left things in a crappy way with Max and now my stomach hurt from it. I could feel Max in my body and in my brain. Since the human body is made up of so much water, it made sense.

Forget science, though. Even if I was only 1 percent water, Max would have had a massive effect on me. I hate to say this, but science had no place in my heart at that moment. It couldn't explain what had happened to me or what I had seen. I knew what I had seen and what I had felt.

My eyes filled with tears, but I looked up to the sky and blinked them back. I stared down at my hands. They were shaking. But another feeling came to the surface and I sort of whispered it to myself.

"I'm so lucky."

Who was I before this trip? What would have happened had I never stepped off this ferry? Did so many people go through life without meeting someone special and sweet and truly magical?

How lucky I felt.

I was incredibly sad, but I was smiling through my tears—a smile I knew I could get back, no matter how low my life got.

There was another life out there.

Another person.

A whole different world.

I moved to the railing and stared down at the water until the tiny ripples went out of focus. Concentrating on something and nothing, the blurry image of the moving water was like meditation, I guess. I let my mind wander with one word repeating itself.

Lucky.

Lucky.

I'm so lucky.

I slid into a minor trance, but something broke it. My eyes came back into focus when I noticed something new in the moving water below me.

A hand came into focus and I watched as it emerged from

the water to clutch the back of the moving ferry with great strength.

I squinted in disbelief and watched in shock as Max's head broke the surface of the water. He shook his hair and focused on me. He had a very calm face, and that heart-exploding tiny smile.

He held onto the back of the ferry with ease and just looked into my eyes. After yet another mega-long staring contest, we both finally broke into laughter—a nervous and relieved laughter on my part. I could now leave the island feeling like I had a real goodbye. A proper one that didn't leave a pain in my stomach or give me a headache. A goodbye for Max that would be sweet and awesome and honor our time together. A goodbye that would let me fall asleep without running all my mistakes through my head over and over.

Max climbed his way up to the deck. True to form, he was wearing only his swimsuit. No shoes, no shirt, no cell phone. Just Max.

We walked slowly to each other and he looked down at his feet. I didn't waste much time. I had to kiss him. After we kissed, he hugged me so hard that I had to exhale with laughter.

We were both alive and together. It didn't matter that I was hours away in the city; this seemed like such a minor thing. We'd figure out the future later.

I thought to myself, *I will remember this feeling when I'm seventy years old. I'll remember this forever.*

"Sorry I'm late. I had to find something," Max said. I didn't respond, but I looked him in the eye. He looked down at his hand and uncurled it.

My spoon necklace.

The one he had made for me. The one that George had thrown into the lake.

I studied the necklace as I held it in my hand. Max snatched it back from me and shoved it playfully in his pocket.

"What did you do that for?" I asked.

"Can I bring it to you later?" he asked, not answering me.

"In the city?" I asked.

"Why not?" he asked.

"How are you going to get to the city?"

"There are tons of rivers from here to there, right?"

"You're back to answering my questions with questions," I teased.

"You want an answer that's not a question?" he asked.

"Yes!" I said and we both laughed.

"I'll swim. I'll swim to you," he said. I blushed at the thought of him doing that. It was too much.

"You didn't answer that question with a question," I finally said. Max thought about this for a second and gave me a smile.

"Was I supposed to?" he asked.

Acknowledgments

Thank you for reading, critiquing, encouraging, or inspiring.

Fabian Garcia Alvarado
Nathan Anderson
Nick Bain
Wade Barry
Raoul Benavides
Melissa Brandt
Ada Brown
Jeffrey Dunn
Andy Froemke
Megan Huber
Juniper Huber Scheife
Brien Kelly
Christian Langheinrich
Chris Lee
The Loughlins
Kari Luoma
Simón Martinez
Heather Meix
Molly Miller
Sally Miller
Bud Nelson
Brian Perry
Molly Reisman
Ryan Scheife
Andrew & Suzanne Stenerson
Maurice Stenerson
Jody Wenner
J. Wery
Jeremy Wilker

62214873R00102

Made in the USA
Lexington, KY
01 April 2017